External Deficits
and the Dollar

External Deficits and the Dollar
The Pit and the Pendulum

RALPH C. BRYANT
GERALD HOLTHAM
PETER HOOPER
Editors

THE BROOKINGS INSTITUTION
Washington, D.C.

Library of Congress Cataloging-in-Publication data:

External deficits and the dollar : the pit and the pendulum / Ralph C. Bryant, Gerald
  Holtham, Peter Hooper, editors.
    p.   cm.
  Based on a workshop held at the Brookings Institution, Jan. 20, 1987.
  Includes bibliographies and index.
  ISBN 0-8157-1146-8   ISBN 0-8157-1145-X (pbk.)
  1. Balance of payments—United States. 2. Balance of trade—United States.
I. Bryant, Ralph C., 1938– . II. Holtham, Gerald. III. Hooper, Peter, 1947– .
IV. Brookings Institution.
HG3883.U7E95   1988   87-27214
382.1′7′0973—dc19   CIP

9 8 7 6 5 4 3 2 1

THE BROOKINGS INSTITUTION is an independent organization devoted to nonpartisan research, education, and publication in economics, government, foreign policy, and the social sciences generally. Its principal purposes are to aid in the development of sound public policies and to promote public understanding of issues of national importance.

The Institution was founded on December 8, 1927, to merge the activities of the Institute for Government Research, founded in 1916, the Institute of Economics, founded in 1922, and the Robert Brookings Graduate School of Economics and Government, founded in 1924.

The Board of Trustees is responsible for the general administration of the Institution, while the immediate direction of the policies, program, and staff is vested in the President, assisted by an advisory committee of the officers and staff. The by-laws of the Institution state: "It is the function of the Trustees to make possible the conduct of scientific research, and publication, under the most favorable conditions, and to safeguard the independence of the research staff in the pursuit of their studies and in the publication of the results of such studies. It is not a part of their function to determine, control, or influence the conduct of particular investigations or the conclusions reached."

The President bears final responsibility for the decision to publish a manuscript as a Brookings book. In reaching his judgment on the competence, accuracy, and objectivity of each study, the President is advised by the director of the appropriate research program and weighs the views of a panel of expert outside readers who report to him in confidence on the quality of the work. Publication of a work signifies that it is deemed a competent treatment worthy of public consideration but does not imply endorsement of conclusions or recommendations.

The Institution maintains its position of neutrality on issues of public policy in order to safeguard the intellectual freedom of the staff. Hence interpretations or conclusions in Brookings publications should be understood to be solely those of the authors and should not be attributed to the Institution, to its trustees, officers, or other staff members, or to the organizations that support its research.

Foreword

THE BLOATED deficits in the U.S. federal budget and in the current account of the U.S. balance of payments have become the dominant macroeconomic problems of the American economy in the last years of the 1980s. The U.S. external deficit—mirrored by large external surpluses in Japan, Germany, and some other countries—is in fact a major problem for the world economy. If the U.S. debt to foreigners continues to mount on the scale of recent years, world economic stability will eventually be threatened. Moreover, the payments deficits ("the pit") have been and may well continue to be accompanied by large swings ("the pendulum") and short-run volatility in the exchange value of the U.S. dollar.

In January 1987, a group of U.S. and foreign economists concerned with these issues met for a workshop at the Brookings Institution. The workshop participants compared empirical analyses of the U.S. external deficit in a search for improved understanding of its causes and cures. Their work was part of a long-term research program on macroeconomic interactions and policy design in interdependent economies, jointly sponsored by Brookings and the Centre for Economic Policy Research in London. As explained in the Introduction to this volume, the workshop was a sequel to a major conference held in March 1986, the proceedings of which are being published by Brookings in *Empirical Macroeconomics for Interdependent Economies*.

This book contains the most important papers and research materials prepared for the January 1987 workshop. Ralph C. Bryant is a senior fellow in the Brookings Economics Studies program. Gerald Holtham, formerly a visiting fellow at Brookings, is now on the staff of Credit Suisse First Boston in London. Peter Hooper is assistant director in the Division of International Finance at the Federal Reserve Board.

The editors and authors have received helpful comments from colleagues at the Brookings Institution and the Federal Reserve. Barbara Koremenos provided research and editorial assistance, and Michelle J. Link and Kenneth P. Pucker also assisted with the research. Evelyn M. E. Taylor and Ruby M. Brooks provided secretarial assistance. The risk of factual error was minimized by Victor M. Alfaro. Jeanette Morrison, Brenda B. Szittya, and Nancy D. Davidson edited the manuscript. Diana Regenthal prepared the index.

The workshop and this book have received generous financial support from the Ford Foundation.

The views expressed here are those of the authors and editors and should not be attributed to the Ford Foundation, the Board of Governors of the Federal Reserve System, or the officers, trustees, or other staff members of the Brookings Institution.

BRUCE K. MAC LAURY
President

November 1987
Washington, D.C.

Contents

Text Tables

Annex Tables

Text Figures

Annex Figures

CHAPTER ONE

Introduction

RALPH C. BRYANT, GERALD HOLTHAM,
AND PETER HOOPER

THE CURRENT-account balance in the U.S. balance of payments, which
showed a surplus of $2 billion in 1980, ballooned to an unprecedented
deficit of more than $140 billion in 1986.[1] During the period from 1980
through early 1985, the dollar nearly doubled in exchange value against
major foreign currencies. Then between early 1985 and the spring of
1987, the dollar swung sharply down, reversing most of its increase in
value over the preceding five years. Despite the swing back of the dollar
pendulum in 1985–87, the massive external deficit persisted.

Early in the decade, the mounting deficit and the strengthening dollar
received little public attention. Policymakers and analysts focused on
domestic issues such as the budget deficit of the federal government. As
the external deficit grew, however, pushing the United States into a net
debtor position for the first time since 1914, public interest was gradually
awakened. By 1987, the external deficit and the dollar were central
economic issues, capturing as much public attention as the budget
deficit.

One reason for the mushrooming of concern was the novelty of the
economic situation. The country that had endured two world wars and
several episodes of severe economic turbulence by relying primarily on
its own resources was now becoming increasingly beholden to foreigners
for its economic well-being.

Suddenly, spokespersons from many different fields pronounced
strong views. The causes of the external deficit were in dispute. For
example, a senior administration official asserted that the root of the

---

1. This imbalance in the current account—referred to in this book as the U.S.
external deficit—is the net sum of transactions in goods, services, investment income,
and transfer payments between U.S. residents and foreigners. The largest part of the
current-account deficit is the trade deficit (the shortfall of merchandise exports below
merchandise imports).

1

problem was a deep-seated loss of nonprice competitiveness by American business. Others blamed unfair trading practices of foreigners. And, of course, cures were addressed. Members of Congress, journalists, and others were fearful that the depreciation of the dollar would have little effect on the external deficit. In trade unions and some academic circles, it was claimed that changes in U.S. trade, commercial, and industrial policies were necessary. The drive for protectionism, never absent in an era of high unemployment, intensified. A bill seeking to pressure foreigners' trade practices into conformity with American preferences passed the House of Representatives in 1986. Similar bills were before both the House and the Senate in 1987. Some trade legislation seemed probable, with the reluctant acquiescence of the administration.

In such an atmosphere, it is important to inject as much fact and analysis into the debate as can be mustered. First, the causes of the external deficit must be carefully assessed. Can factors such as the appreciation of the dollar and the relatively fast growth of the U.S. economy earlier in the decade adequately explain the deficit, or is it necessary to resort to other possible explanations like increased foreign protectionism or structural changes in some of the world's economies? Given one's answers to questions about causes, the implications for the future must be considered. Will the external deficit continue to grow or will the depreciation of the dollar since 1985 be sufficient to erase it? Finally, are there additional policy measures that should be undertaken by the U.S. and foreign governments to mitigate the problem? This book addresses these questions.

Origin of the Study

On January 20, 1987, a workshop on the U.S. current-account imbalance was held at the Brookings Institution. The workshop aspired to improve understanding of the reasons for the deficit and to specify policy options for correcting it. The workshop was a continuation of a research program that has been under way at the Brookings Institution since early 1985. Entitled "Macroeconomic Interactions and Policy Design for Interdependent Economies," the program has been a joint venture by Brookings and the Centre for Economic Policy Research in London and is financed by a grant from the Ford Foundation.

One part of the program strives to compare the properties of multi-country econometric models and to determine whether enough consensus exists in the estimates of the models to provide a reasonable basis for economic policymaking. In March 1986, for example, Brookings held a conference that compared the results of twelve different multicountry models in a set of uniform simulation experiments.[2] Economists from a number of countries analyzed these results, considered whether there were any policy lessons to be learned, and identified avenues for further empirical research.

The current-account sectors, key parts of the international linkages in the models, were identified as meriting more intensive empirical analysis. Moreover, a study of the U.S. current-account deficit and its sensitivity to swings in the dollar seemed especially pertinent given the developments of the 1980s and the policy attention the issue was generating by 1987.

Thus, using the network of model groups already established, participants representing models with sufficiently detailed specifications of the U.S. current account were invited to take part in the workshop. At the same time, two papers were commissioned from economists with research interests in the area. Participants in the January 1987 workshop included individuals responsible for the construction and operation of the following econometric models: the Data Resources Inc. model of the U.S. economy (DRI), the World Econometric Model of the Japanese Economic Planning Agency (EPA), the Multicountry Model of the Federal Reserve Board staff (MCM), the Global Economic Model of the National Institute of Economic and Social Research in London (NIESR GEM), the Interlink Model System of the OECD's Economic and Statistics Department (OECD), the multicountry model of John Taylor (TAYLOR), and the International Model of Wharton Econometric Associates (WHARTON).

Design of the Study

From its conception, the study was designed to be both retrospective and prospective. Looking backward, the researchers sought to determine

2. In addition to a baseline, there were seven forward-looking simulations representing unanticipated shocks—for example, a foreign fiscal expansion—and covering the period 1985–90. The variables reported typified the consequences of the various shocks for the U.S. economy, the exchange value of the U.S. dollar, and economic activity and inflation in the rest of the world. Ralph C. Bryant and others, eds., *Empirical Macroeconomics for Interdependent Economies* (Brookings, forthcoming), reports the results and proceedings of the conference.

whether any kind of consensus exists about explanations for the current-account imbalance and then to examine the relative importance of each of several factors that worked to widen the deficit. Looking forward, the researchers explored the probable evolution of the current-account balance under existing policies and then considered how changes in policies might alter that evolution.

To focus the study, the participating modeling groups were asked to disengage the U.S. current-account sectors from the rest of their models. Hence, key determinants of the current account, such as the exchange value of the dollar and U.S. and foreign incomes and prices, were treated as predetermined rather than as endogenous variables. For this study, in other words, such variables were fixed on commonly assumed paths. In full-model simulations, in contrast, such variables would endogenously respond to policies and to other exogenous shocks.

Of course, the way policies and other exogenous shocks influence incomes, prices, and exchange rates is itself a crucial topic for analysis. The results of the March 1986 Brookings conference, however, showed that the models differ substantially in the way they characterize and predict such influences. Differences among the models in their predictions of these fundamental influences, if not controlled for, would have seriously clouded the effort to assess consensus about the proximate determination of the current account. Thus, for the purposes of this study, the current-account sectors were divorced from the rest of the models, thereby permitting full concentration on the current account and its sensitivity to the dollar and other explanatory variables.

It is a disadvantage of "partial" simulations that they ignore potentially important indirect effects. Feedback effects to the fixed, explanatory variables are overlooked. For example, changes in imports and exports, attributable in part to a change in U.S. income, could in turn influence income. Such feedbacks, which are neglected in partial simulations, could be significant. Hence, it is important to use caution when drawing broad policy implications from the experiments reported here.

The first set of simulations prepared for the workshop examined the historical performance of current-account equations. Given their equations for the volumes of exports and imports and the corresponding trade prices in their models, model groups were asked to "predict" the current account, real net exports, and their major components for 1980–86. Answers to two questions were sought. Could the current-account blocks in the models reproduce the actual movements in trade and services given the behavior of demand and exchange rates? If there were residuals, were they attributable to exports or imports, prices or volumes?

The next set of experiments focused on specific current-account determinants. Sensitivity tests were conducted in which explanatory variables were "shocked" one at a time and the effects on the current-account variables of interest were recorded. Results were expressed as deviations from a base case defined over a period of five years. The shock experiments focused on changes in incomes and prices, both U.S. and foreign, and on two types of exchange rate changes. For example, one of the experiments asked how the volumes and prices of U.S. exports and U.S. imports would change if the dollar depreciated by 20 percent against the Japanese yen and the currencies of the European Monetary System on the hypothetical assumption that all other variables determining the U.S. current account remained unchanged.

A further experiment required model groups to prepare a projection of the current account and its components over 1987–91 on the basis of common assumptions about economic growth, prices, and changes in exchange rates. The projection, termed scenario A, was of course entirely contingent on the assumptions; the projection was not a forecast. Two issues were under consideration. Did any consensus exist across the models on the prospects for a reduction in the external deficit? If so, what were the main features of that consensus?

The remaining materials prepared for the workshop postulated two alternative scenarios. Each alternative was again a conditional projection, not a forecast. The first of these, scenario B, postulated a reduction of the U.S. fiscal deficit and an acceleration in U.S. money supply growth relative to the baseline in scenario A. The second alternative, scenario C, postulated changes in the policies of both the U.S. and foreign governments; scenario C combined the U.S. policies of scenario B with foreign fiscal and monetary stimulus.[3] The alternative scenarios were designed to shed light on the topical issue of whether changes in policies, and if so which changes, could bring about a satisfactory evolution of the U.S. external deficit.

The detailed results of these various experiments, which were presented and evaluated at the Brookings workshop, are presented in the Annex of this volume. The results are presented in the form of tables

3. The assumed paths for incomes, prices, and exchange rates in scenarios B and C were prepared by using an average of the simulation results from the March 1986 Brookings conference.

and figures. Preceding the results for each of the experiments is a summary of the instructions followed by the model groups when preparing that particular experiment. In addition, the Annex provides a listing of the key parameter values (for example, income and price elasticities) for each of the models.[4]

Overview

In addition to the background materials in the Annex, this volume contains three papers prepared in association with the workshop. Chapter 2, "An Empirical Analysis of the External Deficit, 1980–86," by William L. Helkie and Peter Hooper, and chapter 4, "Sustainability and the Decline of the Dollar," by Paul R. Krugman, are revised versions of papers presented at the workshop. Chapter 3, "The U.S. External Deficit: Diagnosis, Prognosis, and Cure," by Ralph C. Bryant and Gerald Holtham, was prepared after the workshop to highlight the workshop's main conclusions. The views presented in chapters 2 through 4, it should be stressed, are those of their authors and do not necessarily reflect the views of the other workshop participants.

Helkie and Hooper's discussion in chapter 2 is primarily retrospective. It presents an empirical analysis of the factors that contributed to the widening of the U.S. external deficit between 1980 and 1986. The paper first presents a recently estimated empirical model of the current account (which corresponds closely to the current-account block of the U.S. model in the Federal Reserve's Multicountry Model—MCM) and reviews its performance in "predicting" historical movements in the current account. That model is then used to assess the relative importance of changes in U.S. price competitiveness and changes in U.S. and foreign growth as determinants of the deficit. Helkie and Hooper find that, while growth factors were significant, the decline in U.S. competitiveness brought about by the appreciation of the dollar was the dominant cause of the widening of the deficit.

Helkie and Hooper's analysis is also pursued at a more fundamental level, using simulation results from several multicountry models to

---

4. More detail on the specification of each participating model and on how experiments were conducted can be found in "Workshop on the U.S. Current-Account Imbalance: Model Memoranda," Brookings Discussion Papers in International Economics 59-A and 59-B, March 1987.

assess the influence of the ultimate causes of changes in the dollar and relative growth rates. They find that shifts in U.S. and foreign fiscal policy can account for over half of the widening of the U.S. external deficit, though such shifts explain only part of the rise in the dollar. A significant role must also be assigned to monetary policy. The external deficit is, therefore, substantially a macroeconomic phenomenon.

Given the importance of the dollar's appreciation as a cause of the widening of the deficit, Helkie and Hooper ask why the deficit has apparently been so slow to respond to the dollar's decline in real terms since early 1985. They conclude that the apparent delay can be attributed largely to normal lags in the response of trade prices to exchange rate changes and to further lags in the response of trade volumes to prices, although there is some evidence that the lags have lengthened in recent years. Moreover, the real net export deficit would have widened substantially further during 1986 and 1987 in the absence of the depreciation.

In chapter 3, Bryant and Holtham briefly review the causes of the ballooning external deficit. Their summary of the historical simulations prepared by the model groups, which is consistent with and reinforces the conclusions reached by Helkie and Hooper, stresses that there is little mystery about the recent history of the U.S. current account. The causes of the external deficit are chiefly macroeconomic.

Bryant and Holtham then focus on the prospective evolution of the deficit. Drawing on the results of the simulation experiments, they predict that the 1985–87 fall of the dollar will lead to a moderate improvement in the external balance in 1987 and to a larger improvement in 1988. The contribution to the growth of U.S. gross national product resulting from the improvement in real net exports could amount to 1 percent a year in 1987–88. Nonetheless, the dollar depreciation as of mid-1987 is unlikely, in their view, to hold the current-account deficit below $100 billion. By 1989, given the policies being pursued in 1987, the deficit is likely to deteriorate anew—partly because of growing net interest payments to foreigners consequent on the growing external debt. Still more depreciation beyond the level of mid-1987, therefore, is probably needed to eliminate the deficit.

Yet further depreciation of the dollar, they argue, is unlikely to be effective on its own. In fact, its inflationary effects in the United States and deflationary effects abroad could be harmful to the world's economies. Macroeconomic policy changes are required, including further fiscal restriction in the United States and expansionary policies in other countries. Bryant and Holtham stress that such policy measures would not be substitutes for further dollar depreciation; rather, they would be needed to ensure that a further depreciation would be effective.

Bryant and Holtham criticize the "Group of Six" agreement of February 1987. The announced policy changes were not sufficient to validate the then-current exchange rates of the dollar against major currencies. The commitment to defend those rates could involve an inappropriate tightening of monetary policy in the United States. Bryant and Holtham argue against that and instead urge renewed international negotiations to arrive at a viable set of cooperative macroeconomic policies.

Paul Krugman, in chapter 4, investigates the notion of the "sustainability" of an exchange rate. According to Krugman, a currency "must" decline fast enough to keep debt accumulation within the limits of feasibility. If the real interest rate that a country pays on its external debt exceeds that country's rate of growth, then the debt grows ever larger relative to the ability to repay. Such debt accumulation is not feasible. How fast the exchange market "expects" the currency to decline can be measured by the differential between interest rates on assets denominated in the currency and rates on similar assets denominated in other currencies. Krugman states that, when an exchange rate must decline faster than the exchange market currently expects it to decline, an exchange rate can be judged unsustainable. Krugman develops an algebraic test to determine when an exchange rate is sustainable. He applies that test to both the historical peak of the dollar at the beginning of 1985 and the circumstances of spring 1987.

Krugman notes that, by late 1986, the dollar had depreciated almost to its early 1980 level, and the real interest differential had disappeared. Yet according to virtually all estimates made at that time, including the simulations prepared for the Brookings workshop, the decline in the dollar was not expected to eradicate the external deficit. The current-account balance was predicted to improve modestly for a couple of years but then to worsen again by 1989. On the basis of his criteria, Krugman concludes that the dollar's exchange rate at the end of 1986 was clearly unsustainable. He regards the sharp fall that occurred during January 1987 as a belated recognition by the market of the fundamentals and a confirmation of his analysis. Nevertheless, according to Krugman, the depreciation of the dollar that occurred in early 1987 may still not be enough to put the exchange rate in a sustainable range.

Concluding Observation

In a period when macroeconomic analysis is beset by controversy and even schism, the Brookings workshop on the U.S. current-account imbalance was a modestly heartening occasion. It is only necessary to glance at the results of the simulation experiments to see that the model groups were not unanimous about either the past or the future—especially the future beyond a two-year horizon. Yet the results were not so diverse as to prevent some broad conclusions from emerging.

The U.S. external deficit can be explained by macroeconomic causes, largely by macroeconomic policy. And it is not likely to disappear as a result of the depreciation of the dollar between early 1985 and mid-1987. At the time of the workshop, the public considered neither conclusion self-evident.

There would certainly not be unanimity among participants and observers about the policy implications of those conclusions. But even in the policy domain, there would surely be a large measure of agreement—more than would have prevailed a few years ago and, one may hope, more than would have prevailed had the workshop not been held.

CHAPTER TWO

An Empirical Analysis
of the External Deficit, 1980–86

WILLIAM L. HELKIE AND PETER HOOPER

THIS CHAPTER presents an empirical analysis of the unprecedented growth of the U.S. external deficit during the first half of the 1980s. The analysis is pursued at two levels. First, using a partial-equilibrium current-account model, we consider the relative importance of price competitiveness and comparative U.S.-foreign gross national product growth as causes of the deficit. Then, at a more fundamental level, we draw on the results of international macroeconomic model simulations (obtained from some of the multicountry models used in the March 1986 Brookings conference described in the Introduction) to consider the effect of shifts in fiscal policies in the United States and other industrial countries on the U.S. external deficit.

The results of the analysis indicate that the decline in U.S. price competitiveness associated with the appreciation of the dollar was the dominant partial-equilibrium factor underlying the widening of the deficit. Other factors, including a somewhat faster rate of growth in the United States than abroad, also contributed significantly. More fundamentally, according to the model simulations, both fiscal expansion in the United States and fiscal contraction abroad were significant causes, probably accounting for over half of the rise in the deficit, with the U.S. fiscal policy shift having the more important effect. But the shifts in

The authors are staff members in the Division of International Finance at the Federal Reserve Board. The views expressed here should not be attributed to the Board of Governors of the Federal Reserve System. The paper benefits from comments and suggestions provided at international macroeconomic workshops at the Federal Reserve Board and the Department of Economics at MIT, as well as comments on earlier drafts by Ralph C. Bryant, Gerald Holtham, David H. Howard, Paul R. Krugman, Catherine L. Mann, Larry J. Promisel, and Edwin M. Truman. Michelle Link provided valuable research assistance.

fiscal policy leave much of the real appreciation of the dollar unexplained. Also important was the tightening of U.S. monetary policy in 1979, which probably contributed significantly to the initial run-up in U.S. real interest rates and, consequently, the dollar. The dollar's continuing rise in 1984, however, when U.S. real rates were falling relative to those abroad and when the current account had already fallen substantially into deficit, appears to have been due to speculative behavior and not to economic fundamentals.

Given the importance of the decline in U.S. price competitiveness to the widening of the U.S. deficit, it is reasonable to ask why the deficit has responded so slowly to the dollar's sharp decline since early 1985. Among the explanations that have been offered are that the dollar has not declined much overall, because it has not fallen against the currencies of developing countries; that it has not declined in real terms, against the yen in particular, because of Japan's relatively high productivity growth in manufacturing; and that foreign firms have cut their profit margins and diminished the gain in price competitiveness to U.S. firms that the falling dollar would otherwise have produced.

We largely discount the first two explanations. The dollar has declined significantly in real terms against a basket of industrial-country and developing-country currencies, and Japanese manufacturing unit labor costs in dollars have risen substantially faster than U.S. unit labor costs since mid-1985. The third explanation is partially true. We have reviewed comparative export price data as well as cost data for the United States, Germany, and Japan. (In 1986 the German and Japanese current-account surpluses combined amounted to about 75 percent of the U.S. deficit, and any significant reduction in the U.S. deficit is likely to involve a significant gain in price competitiveness against those two countries.) The data suggest that Japanese exporters may have been squeezing their profit margins, but that German exporters have not. Indeed, apparent U.S. gains in price competitiveness against German producers have for the most part kept pace with the dollar's depreciation against the mark.

Our own explanation for the delayed response of the U.S. trade balance to the dollar's decline is fourfold. First, profit margins of foreign exporters show considerable but largely transitory flexibility. On average over the past two decades, exchange rates have influenced U.S. import prices with a total distributed lag of about eight quarters. Margins may have been squeezed more in the recent episode than in the past. Second, both import and export volumes lag two years or more in response to price changes, reflecting both recognition-response lags and order-delivery lags. Third, the dollar's decline, which began in mid-March 1985, followed an equally sharp rise during 1984 and early 1985. Because of the lags, the continuing effects of the earlier rise appear to have offset gains due to the dollar's decline at least through mid-1986. Past empirical relationships suggested that U.S. real net exports would begin to respond positively to the depreciation in late 1986 (as they did) and that the nominal trade balance would begin to adjust, though less significantly, in 1987. And, fourth, import prices rise before import volumes fall—the J-curve.

We begin with a brief review of the recent history of the U.S. external position. We then present an empirical model of the U.S. current account, review its recent predictive performance, and provide an accounting of the contribution of proximate determinants to the current-account deficit. Next, we consider the predictions of a group of empirical multicountry models about the effect of U.S. and foreign fiscal policies on the U.S. external deficit. Finally, we review data on U.S. price competitiveness during the dollar's appreciation and subsequent depreciation over the past six years.

Recent History

As indicated in the top half of figure 2-1, the United States ran a small net current-account surplus on average during the three decades before 1980. The decline in the current account to a $141 billion deficit in 1986 is clearly unprecedented in postwar history. Even when scaled for increases in economic activity (nominal GNP), as shown in the bottom panel of figure 2-1, the recent decline is well outside previous postwar experience.

The implications of the deficit for U.S. net external indebtedness are shown in figure 2-2. The solid line shows the officially recorded external investment position (the level of U.S. assets held abroad minus foreign assets held in the United States), and the dashed line shows movements in the cumulative current account.[1] By either measure the U.S. external

1. The difference between the two series reflects movements in the statistical discrepancy, or unreported transactions, in the U.S. international accounts, as well as valuation effects (due principally to exchange rate changes) that are included in the solid line but not the dashed line. The solid line in figure 2-2 implicitly treats the

Figure 2-1. *U.S. Current Account, 1948–86*

Billions of dollars

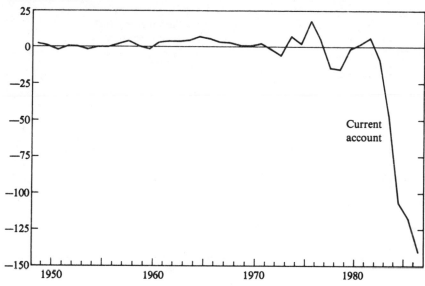

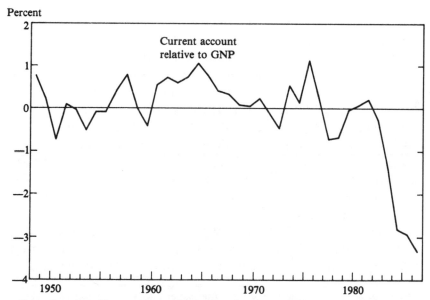

Source: Department of Commerce, Bureau of Economic Analysis, *Survey of Current Business,* various issues.

Figure 2-2. *U.S. External Investment Position, 1948–86*

Billions of dollars

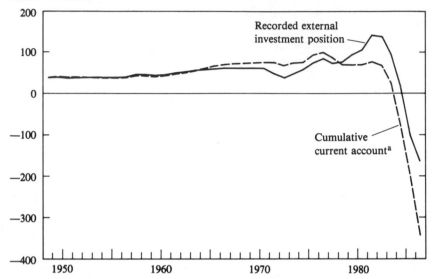

Source: Department of Commerce, BEA, *Survey of Current Business*, various issues.
a. From base of 1948 recorded external investment position.

investment position was substantially positive during most of the past thirty-eight years, contributing to a comfortable surplus on U.S. net investment income receipts, but has turned sharply negative since 1982.

A breakdown of the current-account balance into its major components is given in figure 2-3 and table 2-1. Most of the fall in the current account between 1980 and 1986 reflects the decline in the trade balance (line 13 in table 2-1). Despite the sharp fall in the U.S. net foreign asset position, net investment income (lines 15 and 16) continued to show a healthy surplus because the average rate of return on U.S. assets abroad, of which direct investment is a substantial proportion, is considerably higher than the average rate of return on foreign assets in the United States, which consist largely of claims on banks, Treasury bills, and other portfolio investments. Net portfolio investment income did begin to show a deficit in 1985, but was offset by the positive effects of the dollar depreciation on the valuation of U.S. direct investment income

discrepancy as unreported current-account transactions, while the dashed line implicitly treats it as unreported capital flows. To the extent that the statistical discrepancy reflects unrecorded capital flows, the recorded series (or the solid line in the chart) gives an optimistic picture of the present U.S. external investment position.

Figure 2-3. *Major Components of the U.S. Current Account,
1970–86*

Billions of dollars

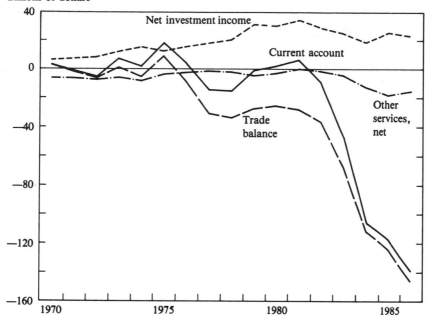

Source: Department of Commerce, BEA, *Survey of Current Business,* various issues.

receipts from abroad. Other net services (line 17), such as military transactions, and travel and transportation services, many of which are sensitive to exchange rates, did begin to decline in 1984. However, the decline was small relative to the overall movement in the current account (line 19).

Table 2-1 also presents some details on movements in the major price and volume components of the merchandise trade balance. As indicated in lines 3 and 9, prices of U.S. nonoil imports and nonagricultural exports showed relatively little net change over this period. A significant rise in the foreign currency prices of U.S. nonoil imports was more than offset by the effects of the net appreciation of the dollar. Meanwhile, U.S. nonagricultural export prices rose only about 3 percent. Almost all of the increase in the trade deficit was accounted for by a doubling of the quantity of nonoil imports between 1980 and 1986 (line 2). Nonagricultural export volume was unchanged (line 8), and agricultural exports fell significantly (line 10). These movements were partly offset by significant

Table 2-1. *Changes in Selected Components of the U.S. Current Account, 1980–86*
Billions of current dollars unless otherwise indicated

Component or balance	1980	1986	Change, 1980–86 Amount	Percent
1. Nonoil merchandise exports, value	170	335	165	97
2. Volume (billions of 1982 dollars)	173	345	. . .	99
3. Price (index, 1982 = 100)	99	97	. . .	−2
4. Oil imports, value	79	34	−45	−58
5. Volume (billions of 1982 dollars)	83	72	. . .	−13
6. Price (index, 1982 = 100)	96	47	. . .	−51
7. Nonagricultural merchandise exports, value	182	197	15	8
8. Volume (billions of 1982 dollars)	202	212	. . .	5
9. Price (index, 1982 = 100)	90	93	. . .	3
10. Agricultural exports, value	42	27	−15	−36
11. Volume (billions of 1982 dollars)	39	30	. . .	−23
12. Price (index, 1982 = 100)	108	90	. . .	−17
13. Merchandise trade balance	−25	−144	−119	. . .
14. Net services	35	19	−16	. . .
15. Net direct investment income	29	31	2	. . .
16. Net portfolio income	2	−10	−12	. . .
17. Other services, net	5	−2	−7	. . .
18. Unilateral transfers	−8	−16	−8	. . .
19. Current-account balance	2	−141	−143	. . .

Source: U.S. Department of Commerce, Bureau of Economic Analysis, *Survey of Current Business*. Value data (lines 1, 4, 7, 10, and 15 through 19) are from table 1 of the U.S. international transactions accounts. The price data (lines 3, 6, 9, and 12) are deflators that are derived from tables 4.3 and 4.4 of the national income and product accounts. The volume data (lines 2, 5, 8, and 11) are derived by dividing the values by their corresponding deflators.

declines in both the price and volume of oil imports (lines 5 and 6). It would be misleading to conclude that the U.S. trade deficit was solely an "import problem," however. Under normal conditions some growth in both imports and exports could be expected. During the early 1980s, nonoil import growth rose substantially above earlier trends, and nonagricultural exports fell substantially below earlier trends.

A breakdown of the changes in U.S. exports and nonoil imports by geographical region is given in table 2-2. Nonoil imports from Japan, other Asian countries, and Western Europe showed the largest increases between 1980 and 1986, especially in percentage terms. Exports to Canada, Japan, and other Asian countries rose somewhat, but shipments to Western Europe and other developing countries fell.

It is clear from the data in table 2-1 that the decline in the trade balance

Table 2-2. *U.S. Trade by Geographical Region, 1980–86*
Billions of dollars

Item	1980	1986	Change, 1980–86	
			Amount	Percent
Nonoil imports	169	335	166	98
Industrial countries	120	238	118	98
Canada	39	66	27	70
Japan	31	81	50	160
Western Europe	43	85	42	98
Other	7	6	−1	−14
Developing countries	49	93	44	90
Latin America	19	31	12	63
Asia	18	46	28	156
Other	12	16	4	33
Exports	217	219	2	1
Industrial countries	138	151	13	9
Canada	42	57	15	36
Japan	21	26	5	24
Western Europe	68	61	−7	−10
Other	7	7	0	0
Developing countries	79	68	−11	−14
Latin America	39	31	−8	−20
Asia	14	17	3	21
Other	26	20	−6	−23

Source: Board of Governors of the Federal Reserve System data base, June 1987.

between 1980 and 1986 was due to a fall in net exports of goods in real terms. The close association between movements in the current account and real net exports of goods, further illustrated in figure 2-4, strongly suggests that an analysis of the decline in the current-account balance should focus on the behavior of import and export volumes. However, one might also ask why the U.S. terms of trade (excluding oil imports and agricultural exports) changed so little between 1980 and 1986 despite the large movement in the dollar's exchange rate over that period. Both of these issues will be addressed later.

Current-Account Model

This section presents the partial-equilibrium current-account model that is used in the next section to calculate the contribution of the major proximate determinants of the U.S. current account to the growth of the

Figure 2-4. *U.S. External Balance, 1978–86*

Billions of dollars

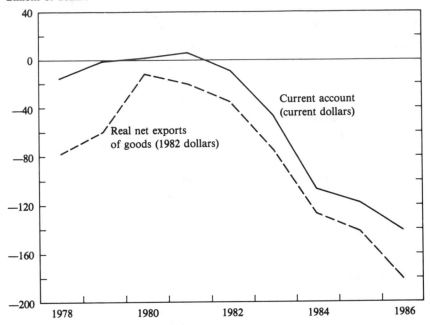

Source: Department of Commerce, BEA, *Survey of Current Business,* various issues.

trade deficit between 1980 and 1986. We begin with brief descriptions of the trade and service account equations, which are presented in implicit functional form in table 2-3, along with definitions of variables. We then describe the model's parameter estimates, discuss some of the dynamics of the model and conclude with an assessment of the model's in-sample and recent post-sample predictive performance.

The model represents an extension of earlier work by Helkie, Helkie and Stekler, and Hooper and is essentially the U.S. current-account sector of the Federal Reserve Board Multicountry Model.[2] In itself the

2. See William L. Helkie, "A Forecasting Model of the U.S. Merchandise Trade Balance," paper presented at the Fifth International Symposium on Forecasting, Montreal, June 1985; Helkie and Lois Stekler, "Model for Forecasting the Services Sector of the U.S. Balance of Payments Accounts," paper presented at the Fourth International Symposium on Forecasting, London, June 1984; Peter Hooper, "Forecasting Export and Import Prices and Volumes in a Changing World Economy," International Finance Discussion Paper 99 (Board of Governors of the Federal Reserve

Table 2-3. *Current-Account Model*[a]

Equations

Merchandise trade

Nonagricultural export volume
1. $X_{na}/P_{xna} = f[\overset{+}{Y^*}, \overset{-}{(P_{xna}/E \cdot P^*)_{L9}}, \overset{-}{K^*/K}, DS]$

Agricultural export volume
2. $X_a/P_{xa} = f[\overset{+}{Y^*}, \overset{-}{(P_{xa}/E \cdot P^*)_{L8}}, \overset{-}{(P/P_{xa})_{L9}}, DS]$

Nonoil import volume
3. $M_{no}/P_{mno} = f[\overset{+}{Y}, \overset{-}{(TR \cdot P_{mno}/P)_{L8}}, K/K^*, CU^*/CU, DS]$

Oil import volume
4. $M_o/P_{mo} = C_o + \overset{+}{I_o} + X_o - Q_o$

5. $C_o = f[\overset{+}{Y}, \overset{-}{(P_{mo}/P)_{L60}}]$

Nonagricultural export price
6. $P_{xna} = f[\overset{+}{PD}, \overset{+}{(P^*/E)_{L4}}]$

Agricultural export price
7. $P_{xa} = f(\overset{+}{Y^*}, \overset{-}{E})_{L8}$

Nonoil import price
8. $P_{mno} = f[\overset{+}{P^*}, \overset{-}{(E)_{L8}}, \overset{+}{(PC)_{L4}}]$

Services

Direct investment income receipts
9. $X_{yd} = f(\overset{+}{Y^*}, \overset{+}{CU^*}, \overset{+}{A_d})$

Direct investment income payments
10. $M_{yd} = f(\overset{+}{Y}, \overset{+}{CU}, \overset{+}{A_d^*})$

Other investment income receipts
11. $X_{yo} = R_{yo} \cdot A_o$

12. $R_{yo} = f[\overset{+}{R}, \overset{+}{(R_{yo}^*)_{L1}}]$

Other investment income payments
13. $M_{yo} = R_{yo}^* \cdot A_o^*$

14. $R_{yo}^* = f[\overset{+}{R}, \overset{+}{(R_{yo}^*)_{L1}}]$

Other service receipts
15. $X_{os}/P_{xos} = f[\overset{+}{Y^*}, \overset{-}{(P_{xos}/E \cdot P^*)_{L8}}]$

Other service payments
16. $M_{os}/P_{mos} = f[\overset{+}{Y}, \overset{-}{(P_{mos}/P)_{L8}}]$

Balances

Merchandise trade balance
17. $TB = X_{na} + X_a - M_{no} - M_o$

Current account
18. $CA = TB + X_{yd} + X_{yo} + X_{os} - M_{yd} - M_{yo} - M_{os} - NT$

Asset stocks
19. $CA = \Delta(A_d + A_o - A_d^* - A_o^*)$

Definitions of variables

A_d	Stock of U.S. foreign direct investment assets	PD	Average of U.S. sectoral price indexes weighted by nonagricultural export shares
A_o	Stock of U.S. other assets (portfolio) abroad	P_{mno}	Nonoil import deflator
CA	Current account	P_{mo}	Oil import deflator
C_o	U.S. oil consumption	P_{mos}	Deflator, other service receipts
CU	Manufacturing capacity utilization	P_{xa}	Agricultural export deflator
DS	Dock-strike variable	P_{xna}	Nonagricultural export deflator
E	Exchange rate (foreign currency–dollar), weighted average[b]	P_{xos}	Deflator, other service payments
		Q_o	U.S. domestic oil production
ΔI_o	Change in U.S. private and government oil stocks	R	U.S. Treasury bill rate
		R_{yo}	Rate of return on U.S. portfolio assets abroad
K	Domestic private fixed capital stock		
$L9$	Subscript denoting, for example, nine-quarter distributed lag on the term in parentheses	TB	Trade balance
		TR	Index of tariff rates
		X_a	Agricultural export value
M_{no}	Nonoil import value	X_{na}	Nonagricultural export value
M_o	Oil import value	X_o	U.S. oil exports
M_{os}	Other service payments (non-investment income)	X_{os}	Other service receipts
		X_{yd}	Direct investment income receipts
M_{yd}	Direct investment income payments	X_{yo}	Other investment income receipts
M_{yo}	Other (portfolio) investment income payments	Y	Real GNP
NT	U.S. net unilateral transfers to foreigners	$*$	Denotes foreign variable (for example, A^* = stock of foreign assets in the United States, R_{yo}^* = rate of return on foreign portfolio assets in the United States, Y^* = foreign GNP).
P	U.S. GNP deflator		
P^*	Foreign CPI, weighted average[b]		
PC	World commodity price		

a. Expected signs of coefficients are listed above variables.
b. E and P^* are weighted differently in different equations, as described in the text.

current-account sector is a two-country model, with the United States and an aggregated "rest of world," although considerable effort is made to take into account the importance of differences among various foreign regions and "third-country" effects in the empirical specification of the equations.

Merchandise Trade Volumes

In the merchandise trade sector, trade volumes other than agricultural exports and oil imports are determined in import demand equations (U.S. exports are treated as foreign imports), with goods produced in the two regions treated as imperfect substitutes. The standard specification, which includes home income and the price of the imported good (measured in home currency) relative to an index of home prices, is augmented in several respects (see equations 1 and 3 in table 2-3).

First, we include a cyclical nonprice rationing variable, the ratio of foreign to home capacity utilization, as developed by R. G. Gregory.[3] This variable proved to be significant only in the U.S. import equation.

Second, we augment the relative price term in both the import and export equations by adding a relative secular supply variable to the equation. Our defense for this unabashedly ad hoc adjustment is that the existing price indexes do not adequately capture the price effects of the introduction of significant new product lines. Japan's entry into the world market as a major producer of passenger cars and other consumer durables beginning in the 1960s and early 1970s, for example, substantially accelerated the growth of U.S. imports during that period. The growth in U.S. imports from newly industrialized countries provides a more recent example. The standard import demand equation tends to capture such developments spuriously as increases in the U.S. income elasticity of demand for imports. Since we view such developments as fundamentally supply-determined, we have chosen to add a proxy for secular shifts in relative output supply. After testing a number of variables, we selected, largely on empirical grounds, the ratio of home

System, December 1976); Hooper, "The Stability of Income and Price Elasticities in U.S. Trade, 1955–77," International Finance Discussion Paper 119 (Board of Governors of the Federal Reserve System, June 1978). For a description of the full MCM, see Hali J. Edison, Jaime R. Marquez, and Ralph W. Tryon, "The Structure and Properties of the FRB Multicountry Model," Economic Modelling, vol. 4 (April 1987), pp. 115–315.

3. R. G. Gregory, "United States Imports and Internal Pressure of Demand: 1948–68," American Economic Review, vol. 61 (March 1971), pp. 28–47.

Table 2-4. *Parameter Estimates for Trade Volume Equations,*
1969:1–1984:4[a]

Independent variable or summary statistic	Nonagricultural exports	Agricultural exports	Nonoil imports	Oil consumption
Intercept	−7.27	0.65	−2.45	−2.07
	(−1.53)	(0.83)	(−0.52)	(−0.77)
Income	2.19	1.15	2.11	1.07
	(5.46)	(12.31)	(5.30)	(5.52)
Relative price	−0.83	−0.93	−1.15	−0.96
	(−6.11)	(−5.87)	(−10.03)	(−2.87)
Relative supply	−1.37	0.54	−0.83	. . .
	(2.27)	(5.07)	(−2.18)	
Dock-strike	0.78	1.07	0.81	. . .
	(8.42)	(3.67)	(5.71)	
Relative capacity utilization	. . .	. . .	−0.28	. . .
			(−1.33)	
Summary statistic				
Rho	0.69	0.19	0.47	0.40
	(7.44)	(1.83)	(4.20)	(3.97)
$\bar{R}^2$	0.89	0.94	0.96	0.93
Standard error of estimate	0.027	0.057	0.031	0.027
Durbin-Watson	2.11	1.87	1.92	1.86

a. Equations are expressed in logarithmic form. Trade in gold and silver is excluded from the dependent variable. Numbers in parentheses are t-statistics.

to foreign productive capital stocks, as proxied by cumulated net fixed investment.

Finally, we added a dock-strike variable developed by Peter Isard, and, to the relative price term, an index of tariff rates.[4]

The coefficient estimates for the U.S. nonoil import and nonagricultural export volume equations are given in table 2-4. These equations were estimated using quarterly data from 1969:1 to 1984:4, in a double-log functional form. In the export equation, foreign GNPs were averaged using each country's or region's share in U.S. nonagricultural exports, while foreign prices and exchange rates were weighted by each country's share in world trade.[5] Multilateral trade weights were used in the latter

4. See Peter Isard, "Dock-Strike Adjustment Factors for Major Categories of U.S. Imports and Exports, 1958–74," International Finance Discussion Paper 60 (Board of Governors of the Federal Reserve System, February 1975). Tariff rate equals tariff receipts obtained from the monthly *Treasury Bulletin* divided by the nonoil import value.

5. Countries represented in the foreign income variable include each major industrial

Table 2-5. *Relative Price and Exchange Rate Lags in Estimated Equations, 1969:1–1984:4*[a]

Lag period	Nonagricultural export volume		Nonoil import volume		Nonoil import deflator		Nonagricultural export deflator	
	Lag coefficient	Cumulative	Lag coefficient	Cumulative	Lag coefficient	Cumulative	Lag coefficient	Cumulative
Current 0	0	0	−0.42	−0.42	−0.28	−0.28	−0.12	−0.11
1	0.06	0.06	−0.30	−0.72	−0.21	−0.49	−0.06	−0.17
2	0.10	0.16	−0.21	−0.93	−0.16	−0.65	−0.03	−0.20
3	0.12	0.28	−0.13	−1.06	−0.11	−0.76	−0.01	−0.21
4	0.14	0.42	−0.07	−1.13	−0.08	−0.84	...	...
5	0.14	0.56	−0.03	−1.16	−0.04	−0.88	...	...
6	0.12	0.68	0	−1.16	−0.02	−0.90	...	...
7	0.10	0.78	0.01	−1.15	−0.01	−0.91	...	...
8	0.06	0.83	...	...	...	...	...	...

a. Exchange rate appears directly in nonagricultural export volume equation and nonoil import deflator equation. Lags are quarterly.

case to take into account the competition that U.S. exports face from many countries in third markets. The estimated income elasticities in the import and export equations are nearly identical, at 2.1 and 2.2, respectively. The long-run price elasticities are both roughly in the neighborhood of -1.0 (-0.8 for exports and -1.05 for imports), suggesting that the Marshall-Lerner condition is met comfortably. We selected eight- to nine-quarter distributed lags in the relative price terms on empirical grounds, after having tested various lag lengths. The actual and cumulated lag coefficient estimates are listed in the first four columns of table 2-5.

These income and price elasticity estimates are crucial to an analysis of the causes of the U.S. current-account deficit. The income elasticities are noteworthy in two respects. First, they contradict the commonly held view that the income elasticity of U.S. imports is significantly greater than that of U.S. exports. We find that the addition of the relative supply proxy has the effect of lowering the import elasticity and raising the export elasticity. In addition, the relative capacity utilization terms in the import equation also tend to lower the income elasticity. In effect the total *cyclical* income elasticity is greater in the import equation, when the relative capacity utilization elasticity of 0.3 is combined with the income elasticity of 2.1, than in the export equation, which does not have a capacity utilization term.

Second, the income elasticities are estimated using real GNP, rather than total domestic expenditure, as the activity variable. This selection has important implications for the partial-equilibrium analysis in the following section. We chose GNP partly because much of U.S. trade is in intermediate products, and there is no reason to believe that inputs into the production of U.S. exports and final goods that compete directly with imports are any less import-intensive than inputs into the rest of U.S. output. To the extent that the import equation represents demand for intermediate goods, real GNP is clearly preferable to a total expenditure variable. In addition, the use of GNP in determining imports of final goods can be readily derived from underlying demand theory.[6] Both

country (members of the Organization for Economic Cooperation and Development and South Africa), plus Mexico and two regions—OPEC and non-OPEC less developed countries (excluding Mexico). In the relative price term, the foreign Group of Ten represents the industrial countries, and eight LDCs (including Mexico, Brazil, Taiwan, Singapore, Hong Kong, South Korea, Philippines, Malaysia) represent the developing countries.

6. See Edward E. Leamer and Robert M. Stern, *Quantitative International Economics* (Allyn and Bacon, 1970), chap. 2.

real GNP and aggregate domestic expenditure variables were tested empirically in our nonoil import volume equation, and the GNP variable yielded a marginally better overall equation fit.[7]

Agricultural exports (equation 2 in table 2-3) are modeled as a function of foreign income, the ratio of agricultural export prices to foreign domestic prices, and the ratio of agricultural export prices to domestic output prices. The third variable is designed to capture, at least in a crude fashion, the supply response of the U.S. agricultural sector to changes in prices relative to U.S. output costs. Oil imports (equations 4 and 5) are determined as the excess of domestic consumption plus exogenous exports and stock changes over exogenous domestic production. Oil consumption is modeled as a function of domestic income with an elasticity near 1.0 and a fifteen-year distributed lag on the relative price of oil that sums to a long-run price elasticity near -1.0.

Trade Prices

Nonagricultural export and nonoil import prices (equations 6 and 8 in table 2-3) are determined in markup equations. The markup over domestic production costs, proxied by domestic output prices, is a lagged function of competing goods prices in the foreign market. The import price equation also includes a world commodity price variable, since nearly 20 percent of these imports can be classified as basic commodities rather than manufactured goods.

Preliminary estimation results suggested that changes in domestic costs in the exporting country are passed through quickly to U.S. import and export prices. Costs are proxied by an average of domestic output prices by sector, weighted by each sector's share in U.S. nonagricultural exports, in the export price equation and by foreign consumer prices, weighted by bilateral nonoil import shares, in the import price equation. Markups or profit margins are assumed to vary, particularly in the short run, in response to changes in prices in the foreign market. On the import side, nonoil import prices respond with a lag to changes in the dollar's exchange rate. And on the export side, nonagricultural export prices respond with a lag to changes in the exchange rate times foreign prices. The coefficient estimates are shown in table 2-6. The lag coefficients,

7. When the nonoil import volume equation was estimated with total domestic expenditure rather than GNP, the capacity utilization coefficient dropped to zero, and the price elasticity fell somewhat.

Table 2-6. *Parameter Estimates for Trade Price Equations*[a]

Independent variable or summary statistic	Nonagricultural exports	Agricultural exports	Nonoil imports
Intercept	−0.15	0.23	4.30
	(−0.34)	(0.56)	(11.33)
Domestic prices	1.05	. . .	. . .
	(10.43)		
Foreign prices[b]	0.21	. . .	0.86
	(3.05)		(19.81)
Exchange rate[b]	−0.21	−0.369	−0.91
	(−3.05)	(−1.91)	(11.34)
Commodity prices[c]	. . .	. . .	0.16
			(3.88)
World GNP	. . .	1.19	. . .
		(2.32)	
Summary statistic			
Rho	0.83	. . .	0.63
	(12.33)	. . .	(6.26)
$\overline{R^2}$	0.97	0.98	0.99
Standard error of estimate	0.011	0.057	0.015
Durbin-Watson	1.65	. . .	1.35

a. Equations are expressed in logarithmic form. Numbers in parentheses are t-statistics.

b. Four-quarter distributed lag on both price and exchange rate in nonagricultural exports; eight-quarter distributed lag on exchange rate in nonoil import equation.

c. *International Financial Statistics* nonoil commodity price index.

given in the last four columns of table 2-5 and illustrated in figure 2-5, imply quite different pricing behavior on the part of U.S. and foreign exporters.

Figure 2-5 shows the responses of nonoil import prices (left-side panels) and nonagricultural export prices (right-side panels) to a hypothetical 10 percent appreciation of the dollar. As indicated in the left-side panels, when the dollar appreciates, foreign exporters raise their home currency prices initially, absorbing most of the exchange rate change into higher profit margins in the near term. Over time, this effect is dissipated as the appreciation is gradually passed through into lower U.S. dollar import prices. Thus, in the short run foreign exporters in the aggregate appear to price to the U.S. market in response to exchange rate changes, but in the longer run, their prices are determined primarily by their domestic costs. The right-side panels show, by contrast, that the home currency (dollar) prices of U.S. exporters change little initially

Figure 2-5. *Effects of Dollar Appreciation on U.S. Nonoil Import Prices and Nonagricultural Export Prices*

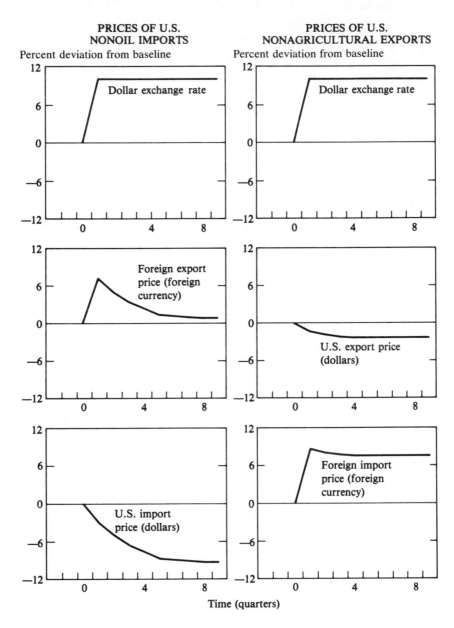

PRICES OF U.S.
NONOIL IMPORTS

PRICES OF U.S.
NONAGRICULTURAL EXPORTS

Percent deviation from baseline

Percent deviation from baseline

Dollar exchange rate

Dollar exchange rate

Foreign export price (foreign currency)

U.S. export price (dollars)

U.S. import price (dollars)

Foreign import price (foreign currency)

Time (quarters)

in response to a change in the exchange rate. Almost all of the dollar appreciation is passed through into higher foreign currency import prices in the foreign market initially (panel 3). U.S. exporters do exhibit some gradual responsiveness to foreign price competition over time, but it is much more subdued than the initial responsiveness of foreign exporters to the same shock.

Services: Investment Income

The investment income equations (equations 9 through 14 in table 2-3) consist of returns on direct investment holdings and interest receipts and payments on financial (portfolio) assets and liabilities.

To determine direct investment receipts and payments we assume that earnings depend on the stock of real direct investment, the price level, and fluctuations in nominal dollar profit rates. We use capacity utilization, the rate of change of GNP, and the price level to represent movements in the rate of profits. The exchange rate is included to translate foreign currency profits into dollars. Because of technical problems regarding definitional consistency in the series, the equation parameters vary substantially as one alters the sample period. In estimation, direct investment receipts were disaggregated into manufacturing, petroleum, and other receipts. (See table 2-7 for the parameter estimates.)

Portfolio interest receipts and payments are determined by an identity that multiplies the implicit interest rate by the value of outstanding assets. We determine the implicit interest rate as a geometric lag of the ninety-day U.S. Treasury bill rate. (The Treasury bill rate is used on the receipts side as well as the payments side because U.S. portfolio claims on foreigners are predominantly dollar-denominated.) In general, given the lagged dependent variables in the equations, changes in the ninety-day Treasury bill rate are almost fully passed through in the long run to changes in implicit interest rates. Parameter estimates are given in table 2-8.

Other Services

Other services, including travel, passenger fares, other transportation, fees and royalties, other private services, and U.S. government miscellaneous services, are aggregated into single equations for both

Table 2-7. *Parameter Estimates for Direct Investment Equations*[a]

Independent variable or summary statistic	Direct investment income receipts			Direct investment income payments
	Manufacturing	Petroleum	Other	
Intercept	2.44	−1.44	−0.86	−2.76
	(1.28)	(−0.61)	(−2.80)	(−2.81)
Capacity utilization	6.42	9.51	3.64	6.60
	(1.98)	(2.45)	(4.49)	(3.35)
Price times real asset stock	0.48	0.88	0.78	0.95
	(2.78)	(3.89)	(27.62)	(9.25)
Price$_t$/price$_{(t-1)}$	2.99	. . .	0.96	. . .
	(3.04)		(1.63)	
Summary statistic				
Rho	0.70	0.75	0.18	0.75
	(6.76)	(7.98)	(1.29)	(10.07)
$\overline{R}^2$	0.63	0.27	0.95	0.55
Standard error of estimate	0.159	0.176	0.082	0.187
Durbin-Watson	2.29	1.85	1.87	2.28

a. Numbers in parentheses are *t*-statistics.

Table 2-8. *Parameter Estimates for the Implicit Interest Rate on Portfolio Investment Income*[a]

Independent variable or summary statistic	Private receipts	Government receipts	Private payments	Government payments
Intercept	0.18	0.07	−0.06	0.03
	(2.83)	(0.72)	(−1.21)	(0.83)
Ninety-day Treasury bill rate	0.50	0.08	0.51	0.19
	(12.53)	(1.30)	(11.83)	(7.93)
Implicit interest rate $(t-1)$	0.45	0.82	0.47	0.80
	(12.38)	(9.35)	(9.81)	(25.61)
Summary statistic				
$\overline{R}^2$	0.98	0.85	0.98	0.99
Standard error of estimate	0.028	0.097	0.049	0.033
Durbin-Watson	2.40	2.75	2.05	2.11

a. Numbers in parentheses are *t*-statistics.

Table 2-9. *Parameter Estimates for Other Services*[a]

Independent variable or summary statistic	Receipts	Payments
Intercept	−3.08	−8.40
	(−9.26)	(−9.27)
Relative price	−0.48	−0.62
	(−9.60)	(−7.88)
Foreign GNP	0.75	. . .
	(14.73)	
U.S. GNP	. . .	0.73
		(5.11)
Real U.S. exports	0.22	. . .
	(5.36)	
Real U.S. imports	. . .	0.27
		(5.25)
Summary statistic		
Rho	0.42	0.58
	(4.07)	(6.14)
$\bar{R}^2$	0.99	0.88
Standard error of estimate	0.017	0.024
Durbin-Watson	2.14	1.84

a. Numbers in parentheses are *t*-statistics.

receipts and payments. Other service transactions are related in general to the same variables that determine merchandise transactions: income and relative prices. We also include real merchandise trade volumes to explain the movements specific to transportation services. Parameter estimates are given in table 2-9.

Balances and Asset Stocks

The deviations of trade and current-account balances from the various components of the model are given in equations 17 and 18 in table 2-3. In full current-account model simulations, asset stocks are endogenized mechanically. An increase in the U.S. current-account deficit, for example, is roughly assumed to be financed half by an increase in foreign portfolio claims on the United States and half by a reduction in U.S. portfolio claims on foreigners. This allows us to take into account feedbacks from shifts in the current account to changes in the net investment income account. The large statistical discrepancy between the current and capital account is treated exogenously.

Predictive Performance

The in-sample (1969–84) and post-sample (1985–86) quarterly predictive performance of the single equations and overall model presented above are shown in figures 2-6 through 2-11. Each figure shows an actual value (solid line), a model prediction (dashed line), and a summary of the in-sample and post-sample percentage root-mean-squared prediction errors. These RMSEs are expressed as percentages of the in-sample or post-sample means, and in the case of balances or net flows as a percentage of the mean sum of the underlying gross flows (for example, total exports plus imports for the trade balance). In order to provide a more stringent test of the predictive power of the structural variables included in the model, autoregressive residuals are not included in the model predictions.

There is little indication of a significant increase in the model's overall prediction error during the post-sample period. In fact, the post-sample errors for real net exports and the current account (see figures 2-10 and 2-11) are below their in-sample means. However, this favorable performance overall masks significant increases in prediction errors for several individual components of the current account. Both the nonoil import and nonagricultural export price equations began to overpredict substantially in 1986 (see figure 2-8). By the fourth quarter of 1986, the import price equation was overpredicting by 5 percent (nearly triple the in-sample RMSE), suggesting that foreign exporters may have been absorbing the effects of the decline in the dollar into their profit margins more than they had previously. The result for export prices would be consistent with just the opposite behavior for U.S. exporters, however. U.S. exporters appear not to have taken advantage of the dollar's fall by raising their dollar prices and profit margins.

While neither the nonoil nor nonagricultural volume equation showed any appreciable increase in prediction error in the recent period (see the top panels of figures 2-6 and 2-7), the equations for the more volatile oil and agricultural components of U.S. trade did (bottom panels of figures 2-6 and 2-7). Oil imports soared in mid-1986 as stocks were being built up in anticipation of a rebound in oil prices, while agricultural exports were depressed in the first half of 1986 in anticipation of a sharp cut in U.S. loan support (and export) prices for various agricultural commodities. (Neither of these price-expectations influences is captured in the model.) A comparison of the first and second panels of figure 2-9 indicates

Figure 2-6. *Actual and Predicted U.S. Import Volume, 1969–86*

Billions of 1982 dollars

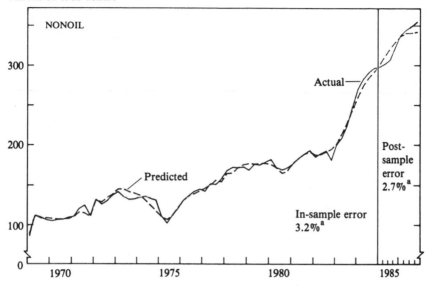

Billions of 1982 dollars

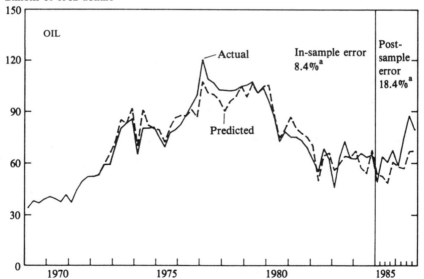

Source: Department of Commerce, BEA, *Survey of Current Business,* various issues. Oil import volume data (on International Accounts basis) not published before 1972.

a. Root-mean-squared prediction error as a percentage of sample mean of actual value.

Figure 2-7. *Actual and Predicted U.S. Export Volume, 1969–86*

Billions of 1982 dollars

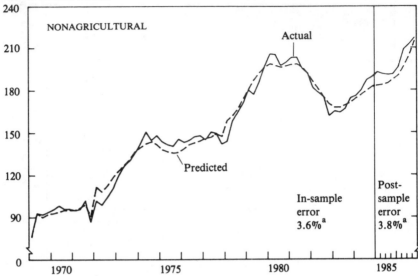

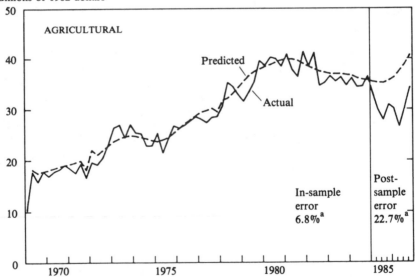

Source: Department of Commerce, BEA, *Survey of Current Business*, various issues.
a. See figure 2-6, note a.

Figure 2-8. *Actual and Predicted U.S. Trade Prices, 1969–86*

Index, 1982 = 100

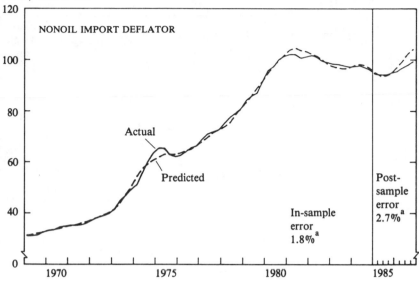

Index, 1982 = 100

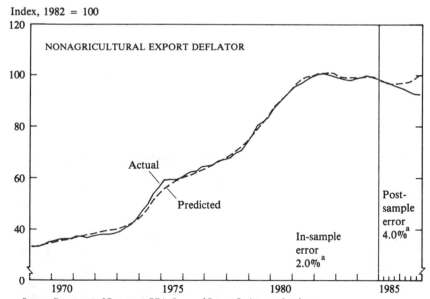

Source: Department of Commerce, BEA, *Survey of Current Business*, various issues.
a. See figure 2-6, note a.

Figure 2-9. *Actual and Predicted U.S. Service Account, 1969–86*

Billions of dollars

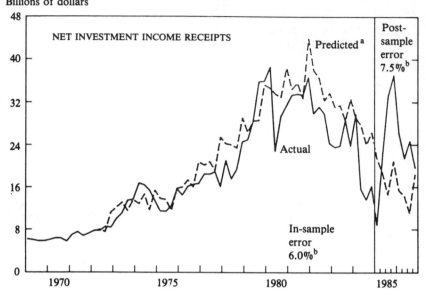

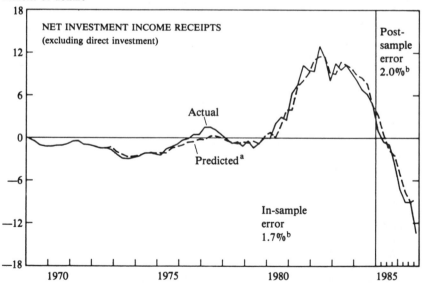

Figure 2-9 *(continued)*

Billions of dollars

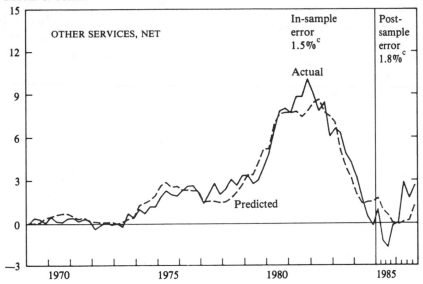

Source: Department of Commerce, BEA, *Survey of Current Business,* various issues.

a. Model prediction of total net investment income receipts not available before 1972 because the direct investment income component of that total was not published before 1972.

b. Root-mean-squared error (RMSE) expressed as percentage of sample mean of gross investment income receipts plus payments.

c. RMSE expressed as percentage of sample mean of total other service receipts plus payments.

that the net direct investment component of net services has become more volatile and difficult to predict in recent years, with much of this volatility probably associated with changes in exchange rates.

Partial-Equilibrium Analysis of the U.S. External Deficit

This section uses the model just described to quantify the contribution of the proximate determinants of the U.S. current account to the growth of the external deficit during the early 1980s.

The changes in the major proximate determinants from 1980 to 1986 are given in table 2-10 (pages 38–39). For exchange rates and other components of relative prices that influence trade volumes with a mean lag of about one year, we also show changes for the period 1979:1–1985:1.

U.S. income and capacity utilization rose somewhat more than their foreign counterparts. U.S. GNP grew about 2 percent more than GNP

Figure 2-10. *Actual and Predicted U.S. External Balance, 1969–86*

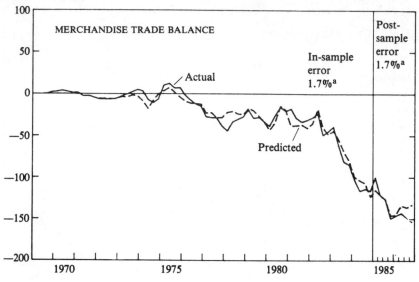

Billions of dollars

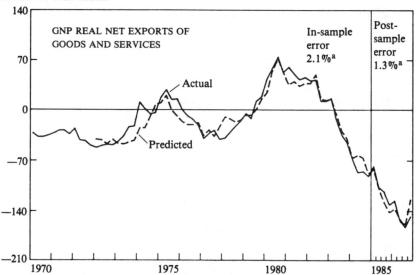

Billions of 1982 dollars

Source: Department of Commerce, BEA, *Survey of Current Business*, various issues.
a. RMSE expressed as percentage of sample mean of total imports plus exports of goods and services.

Figure 2-11. *Actual and Predicted U.S. Current-Account Balance,*
1969–86

Billions of dollars

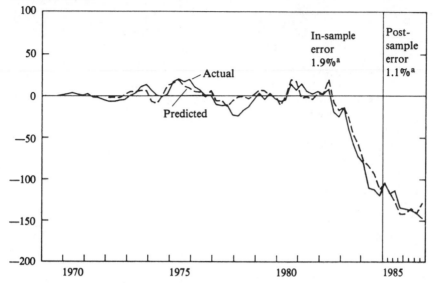

Source: Department of Commerce, BEA, *Survey of Current Business*, various issues.
a. RMSE expressed as percentage of sample mean of total imports plus exports of goods, services, and transfers.

in the rest of the world, with GNP growth in other major industrial
countries averaging more than 0.5 percentage point a year less than the
U.S. growth rate over most of this period and growth in OPEC countries
significantly negative. However, growth in other developing countries
was well above the U.S. rate, paced by a total 1980–86 increase of well
over 30 percent in the GNP of Asian developing countries.

Compared with the relatively small difference between U.S. and total
foreign GNP growth, movements in relative prices were pronounced.
The table includes several measures of foreign prices and exchange
rates, some weighted by multilateral trade shares (for export volume
equations). The overall price and exchange rate indexes are also divided
into their industrial-country and developing-country components. The
latter group includes two high-inflation countries (Brazil and Mexico)
along with six Asian newly industrialized countries. In addition, changes
in the price variables are shown from 1979:1 through 1985:1, the peak in
the dollar, because those variables enter into the determination of import
and export volumes with a significant lag. The distinction between the

Table 2-10. *Changes in Major Determinants of U.S. Current Account, 1980–86 and 1971:1–1985:1*

Determinant	Change	
	1980–86	*1979:1–1985:1*[a]
	Logarithmic percentage change[b]	
1. U.S. real GNP	14.2	. . .
2. Foreign real GNP[c]	12.5	. . .
3. Ten major industrial countries	10.8	. . .
4. Other OECD countries	15.7	. . .
5. Developing countries (excluding OPEC)	20.4	. . .
6. OPEC	−7.6	. . .
7. U.S. capacity utilization	0.7	. . .
8. Foreign capacity utilization[d]	−2.2	. . .
9. U.S. capital stock	16.8	. . .
10. Foreign capital stock[e]	22.3	. . .
11. Relative price of nonoil imports	−30.3	−29.6
12. U.S. GNP deflator	28.9	25.2
13. Nonoil import price	−1.3	−4.4
14. Foreign CPI[f]	64.7	. . .
15. Ten industrial countries	31.7	. . .
16. Eight developing countries	145.5	. . .
17. Exchange rate[f]	50.8	57.7
18. Ten industrial countries	11.4	36.0
19. Eight developing countries	147.5	110.9
20. World commodity price	−31.3	−23.6
21. Relative price of nonagricultural exports	−4.0	29.3
22. Nonagricultural export price	3.2	7.7
23. Foreign CPI[g]	56.8	47.5
24. Ten industrial countries	33.3	30.0

two periods is most important for the relative price of nonagricultural exports, as the depreciation of the dollar between 1985:1 and 1986:4 more than reversed the earlier rise in that relative price.

An analysis of factors contributing to changes in U.S. nonoil import prices and nonagricultural export prices is given in table 2-11. These estimates are based on the model's predictions of the effects of the total change in each of the contributing factors between 1980 and 1986. The results indicate that a large reduction in dollar import prices due to the rise in the dollar was almost exactly offset by a large increase in foreign currency prices due to the rise in domestic prices abroad over the same period. On balance, nonoil import prices fell slightly as world commodity prices made a negative contribution. Meanwhile, nonagricultural export

Table 2-10 *(continued)*

		Change	
	Determinant	*1980–86*	*1979:1–1985:1*[a]
		Logarithmic percentage change[b]	
25.	Eight developing countries	140.7	110.1
26.	Exchange rate[g]	49.5	69.1
27.	Ten industrial countries	24.3	58.1
28.	Eight developing countries	140.5	108.4
29.	U.S. PPI export weights	7.2	...
		Level change	
30.	Treasury bill rate (percentage points)	−5.45	...
31.	U.S. net foreign asset position (billions of dollars)	−275.1	...
32.	Stock of U.S. direct claims on foreigners (billions of dollars)	51.6	...
33.	Stock of U.S. portfolio claims on foreigners (billions of dollars)	391.9	...
34.	Stock of foreign direct claims on United States (billions of dollars)	121.3	...
35.	Stock of foreign portfolio claims on United States (billions of dollars)	597.3	...
36.	Statistical discrepancy (billions of dollars)	143.8	...

Source: FRB U.S. International Transactions (USIT) model data base.

a. For variables that have a lagged impact on the current account.

b. The logarithmic percentage change (for example, in variable X) is calculated as $100 \cdot \Delta \log X$. This measure of change has the advantage of showing quantitatively symmetrical changes for both increases and decreases.

c. Index of real GNP in all OECD countries plus all developing countries (excluding communist countries), weighted by bilateral U.S. nonagricultural export shares.

d. Includes ten major industrial countries, weighted by GNP levels.

e. Includes all OECD countries plus ten developing countries weighted by multilateral trade shares.

f. Includes ten industrial countries and eight major developing countries weighted by bilateral U.S. nonoil import shares.

g. Includes ten industrial countries and eight major developing countries weighted by multilateral trade shares.

prices rose slightly, as the influence of moderate increases in export-weighted U.S. producer prices was partly offset by the net depressing effects of a higher dollar.

It is noteworthy that the increase in the export-share-weighted basket of U.S. producer prices between 1980 and 1986 (line 29 in table 2-10) was only one-fourth as great as the increase in the U.S. GNP deflator (line 12 in table 2-10). To a significant degree this difference reflects the relative importance in U.S. nonagricultural exports of computers and other office machinery, whose domestic prices have been falling at roughly a 10 percent annual rate in recent years.

Table 2-12 presents a partial-equilibrium analysis of factors that contributed to the decline in real net exports of goods between 1980 and

Table 2-11. *Analysis of Factors Contributing to Changes*
in Nonagricultural Export and Nonoil Import Prices, 1980–86

Factor	Logarithmic percentage change in contributing factor	Contribution to change in price index $(1982 = 100)^a$
Nonoil import price	. . .	**−1.3**
Commodity prices	−31.3	−4.8
Foreign CPI	64.7	53.6
Dollar	50.8	−46.6
Residual	. . .	−3.5
Nonagricultural export price	. . .	**3.2**
U.S. wholesale prices	7.2	4.8
Foreign CPI	56.8	11.4
Dollar	49.5	−9.9
Residual	. . .	−3.1

a. Boldface type indicates total change; roman type indicates changes due to contributing factors.

1986. Lines 1 through 15 show estimated contributions of each of the major components of the trade balance, based on the estimated trade volume equations in the model. A summary of the total contribution by type of variable is given in lines 16 through 19. Relative GNP (and capacity utilization) was a significant factor, contributing to about one-fourth of the total growth of the deficit. Despite both the similarity of income elasticities and the relatively small margin by which GNP growth in the United States exceeded GNP growth abroad during this period, growth was still a significant factor because the average scale of U.S. real imports of goods over this period was substantially greater than the scale of exports; hence, even if exports and imports grew at the same rate, imports would grow more in absolute terms.

This estimate of the growth contribution may be understated for a number of reasons. First, the real purchasing power of OPEC and some other developing countries, whose export prices plunged, fell more than would be suggested by the recorded declines in real GNP, which measures actual physical output. Second, estimates based on relative U.S. and foreign growth in domestic demand could show a substantially greater contribution due to growth factors, since the gap between U.S. and foreign domestic demand growth over this period was considerably greater than the gap between U.S. and foreign GNP growth.[8] We believe

8. The decline in U.S. real net exports between 1980 and 1986 amounted to over 5 percent of U.S. real GNP. The same increase in foreign real net exports would amount

Table 2-12. *Analysis of Factors Contributing to Changes in Export and Import Volume, 1980–86*

Factor	Logarithmic percentage change in contributing factor	Contribution to change in trade volume[a] (billions of 1982 dollars)
1. **Nonoil import volume**	. . .	**172**
2. U.S. GNP	14.2	74
3. U.S. capacity utilization/foreign capacity utilization	2.8	2
4. Relative price of U.S. imports	−30.3	85
5. U.S./foreign supply proxy	−5.5	11
6. **Oil import volume**	. . .	**−8**
7. U.S. GNP	14.2	29
8. Conservation and lagged production responses to higher oil prices	. . .	−37
9. **Nonagricultural export volume**	. . .	**7**
10. World GNP	12.5	58
11. Relative price of U.S. exports	4.0	−36
12. U.S./foreign supply proxy	−5.5	−15
13. **Agricultural export volume**	. . .	**−9**
14. World GNP	13.3	5
15. Other factors, net	. . .	−14
16. **Real net exports of goods**	. . .	**−166**
17. Relative GNP growth	. . .	−42[b]
18. Changes in competitiveness	. . .	−157[c]
19. Other factors (mainly oil conservation)	. . .	33[d]

a. Boldface type indicates total change; roman type indicates changes due to contributing factors.
b. Includes lines 2, 3, 7, 10, 14.
c. Includes lines 4, 5, 11, 12 and $10 billion from line 15.
d. Equal to line 16 minus lines 17 and 18.

that the domestic demand approach could have overstated significantly the growth contribution, partly for reasons addressed in the previous section pertaining to the importance of intermediate goods in U.S. trade, and partly because the gap between U.S. and foreign domestic demand growth is likely to have been widened by the direct effects of the dollar's appreciation and the factors underlying that appreciation. However, we also recognize that the gap between U.S. and foreign domestic demand growth was significantly influenced by other factors and that the gap

to a little over 3 percent of GNP in all foreign countries combined. This means that the gap between increases in U.S. and foreign domestic demand (defined as GNP less net exports) would have been more than 8 percentage points greater than the gap between U.S. and foreign GNP increases.

between U.S. and foreign GNP growth was narrowed by the effects of the dollar's appreciation. In this light, our estimates of the partial-equilibrium contribution of growth factors are probably understated to some degree, particularly with respect to the impact on trade in finished goods. This discussion points out the inherent difficulties of trying to allocate causal contributions among jointly determined endogenous variables. The issue clearly warrants further investigation, however, in view of the potentially important policy implications attached to esti-mates of the relative effectiveness of growth measures versus relative price measures as a means of correcting current-account imbalances.

In any event, while the growth factor was significant, our estimates suggest it was clearly dominated by the contribution of the change in competitiveness. The contributions of the changes in relative prices of nonoil imports and nonagricultural exports alone (lines 4 and 11) ac-counted for over three-fourths of the total decline in real net exports. The shift in relative supply proxies (with foreign capital stock growth exceeding U.S. capital stock growth) contributed another $20 billion to the decline. Other factors, including largely the lagged response of U.S. oil consumption and production to the 1979–80 oil price hike (depressing oil imports) worked in the opposite direction to reduce the deficit.

Earlier we noted that the U.S. terms of trade had changed relatively little on balance during 1980–86. In particular, the ratio of nonagricultural export prices to nonoil import prices rose only 6 percentage points. Nevertheless, we find that changes in relative prices associated with the rise in the dollar were the dominant factor underlying the shift in U.S. real net exports of goods. This apparent inconsistency can be explained as follows.

First, the relative price of exports is expressed in terms of foreign currency. As was illustrated in figure 2-5, while the dollar price of U.S. exports falls somewhat following an appreciation (as does the dollar price of U.S. imports), the foreign currency price of U.S. exports *rises* substantially more. Second, the relative price of exports affects export volumes with a mean lag of about one year. Export volumes in the first half of 1986 had been influenced most heavily by relative prices that prevailed in the first half of 1985, before the dollar had fallen significantly (see table 2-10). Finally, the relative price terms include domestic price indexes in their denominators. Although nonoil import prices remained about flat in nominal terms during 1980–86, they fell substantially in real terms, as U.S. domestic prices rose nearly 30 percent during that period.

Table 2-13. *Analysis of Factors Contributing to Predicted Changes in U.S. Net Investment Income Receipts, 1980–86*
Billions of dollars, annual rate

Factor	Change[a]
1. Net service receipts	− 12.7
2. **Net investment income**	**−7.5**
3. **Net portfolio income**	**−11.5**
4. **Receipts**	**16.2**
5. **Government**	**3.8**
6. Asset stock	2.2
7. Interest rate	1.6
8. **Private**	**12.4**
9. Asset stock	31.8
10. Interest rate	− 19.4
11. **Payments**	**27.7**
12. **Government**	**9.8**
13. Asset stock	11.2
14. Interest rate	− 1.4
15. **Private**	**17.9**
16. Asset stock	28
17. Interest rate	− 10.1
18. **Net direct investment income**	**4.0**
19. **Receipts**	**1.9**
20. Asset stock	5.1
21. Foreign capacity utilization	− 9.1
22. Foreign CPI	21.5
23. Exchange rate	− 20.0
24. Other	2.5
25. **Payments**	**−2.1**
26. Asset stock	9.5
27. U.S. capacity utilization	− 0.2
28. U.S. GNP deflator	4.2
29. Other	− 15.6
Memorandum	
30. Total asset stocks	− 9.6
31. Total rates of return	− 17.9
32. Total other	20

a. Boldface type indicates total change; roman type indicates changes due to contributing factors.

Table 2-13 presents an analysis of factors contributing to changes in the net investment income portion of the service account during 1980–86. The table shows changes in total net services and its components, as well as the contributions of various factors to those changes over the six-year period, measured in billions of current dollars at annual rates.

The contributions of changes in assets stocks between 1980 and 1986 were computed at the average rate of return over that period, and the contributions of changes in rates of return at the average level of asset stocks. The asset stocks underlying all of the various receipt and payment categories rose over the period in question, with U.S. liabilities to foreigners (particularly private portfolio liabilities—reflected in line 16) rising substantially more than U.S. claims on foreigners. The overall decline in the U.S. net foreign asset position had a relatively small negative impact on net income receipts, however, as line 30 shows. This is largely because the average rate of return on U.S. private portfolio investments abroad was significantly higher than that on foreign investments in the United States. A substantial portion of U.S. private portfolio liabilities to foreigners is in corporate stocks, whose returns—other than capital gains, which are not included in the investment income accounts—typically are fairly low. Moreover, a large share of U.S. portfolio claims and liabilities represents intermediation by U.S. banks, which typically earn more on their loans and related activities abroad than they pay on their liabilities to foreigners.

The decline in interest rates on private net portfolio receipts (reflected in lines 10, 14, and 17) and the depressing effects of the rise in the dollar on direct investment income receipts both contributed to reductions in U.S. net investment income receipts (line 31). The combined negative impact of changes in asset stocks (line 30) and interest rates (line 31) were partly offset by other factors (line 32), contributing to a $7.5 billion decline in net investment income receipts overall (line 2). Our estimates of factors contributing to direct investment income flows should be taken with caution, however, in view of the large residuals in these equations (reflected in lines 24 and especially 29).

Table 2-14 presents analysis of other service account transactions, including military transactions (which are treated exogenously in the model) and other nonmilitary transactions. The moderate decline in other net services excluding net military receipts (line 3) can be attributed largely to the effects of the dollar's real appreciation (as indicated by the combined effects shown in lines 6, 7, and 13). The net effects of U.S. and foreign growth (lines 5 and 12) were close to zero.

Analysis of Fundamental Determinants

This section draws on the results of multicountry model simulations to assess the contribution of changes in fiscal policies in the United States and abroad to the growth of the U.S. external deficit.

Table 2-14. *Analysis of Factors Contributing to Predicted Changes in Other U.S. Net Service Receipts, 1980–86*[a]

Billions of dollars, annual rate

Factor	Change[b]
1. **Total net service receipts excluding** **investment income**	**−5.2**
2. **Net military receipts**[c]	**−0.2**
3. **Net other service receipts** **excluding military**	**−5.0**
4. **Receipts**	**11.3**
5. Foreign GNP	4.6
6. Foreign CPI	21.6
7. Exchange rates	−20.6
8. U.S. real exports	0.5
9. Other service receipts deflator	3.6
10. Other	1.6
11. **Payments**	**16.3**
12. U.S. GNP	4.0
13. U.S. GNP deflator	6.1
14. U.S. real imports	5.6
15. Other service payments deflator	0.2
16. Other	0.4

a. Net service receipts excluding investment income.
b. Boldface type indicates total change; roman type indicates changes due to contributing factors.
c. Exogenous in the model; therefore has no contributing factors.

Table 2-15 presents several different quantitative estimates of exogenous changes in government budget deficits for the United States and six major foreign industrial countries between 1980 and 1985. The first two columns present International Monetary Fund estimates of structural or cyclically adjusted federal and general (including federal, state, and local) government budget balances. The third column presents the estimate of the Organization for Economic Cooperation and Development for general balances. In principle, these estimates are designed to indicate the overall thrust of exogenous shifts in fiscal policy, with positive numbers denoting contractionary shifts. The IMF and OECD appear to agree that structural general budget balances of the foreign countries moved toward surplus by something on the order of 2.5 percent of GNP between 1980 and 1985. At the same time, the U.S. federal budget balance moved toward deficit by roughly 3.5 percent of GNP. (In the U.S. case, unlike that of most other industrial countries, the federal balance is probably the more appropriate exogenous policy measure.) The growth of the U.S. structural deficit took place fairly steadily over the five-year period.

Table 2-15. *Fiscal Policy: Cumulative Exogenous Changes
in Budget Balances, Canada, France, Germany, Italy, Japan,
United Kingdom, and United States, 1980–85*[a]
Percent of GNP

	IMF estimate		OECD estimate
Country	Central government	General government	General government
Canada	−2.3	−2.9	−3.4
France	0.0	3.2	0.6
Germany	2.9	4.4	3.2
Italy	−0.5	0.8	−2.8
Japan	1.5	3.5	3.6
United Kingdom[b]	3.0	3.8	4.1
Average of six above	1.2	2.8	2.0
United States	−3.7	−2.3	−2.4

Sources: For IMF estimates, see International Monetary Fund, *World Economic Outlook* (Washington, D.C.: IMF, April 1986), pp. 110, 195; OECD estimates are cumulations of changes in structural budget deficits obtained from *OECD Economic Outlook*, various issues from December 1984 to June 1987.

a. A positive number indicates a fiscal contraction, an increase in the structural budget surplus, or a reduction in the structural deficit.

b. Percent of GDP.

Table 2-16 presents a summary of simulations reported by the Federal Reserve Board staff's Multicountry Model (MCM) and an average of nine out of twelve models that participated in the March 1986 Brookings conference.[9] The results of three illustrative simulations are given: a sustained U.S. fiscal contraction equal to 1 percent of baseline GNP, a fiscal expansion in other OECD countries equal to 1 percent of baseline GNP, and a 25 percent nominal depreciation of the dollar against other OECD currencies, on average. The table shows the impact of each of these shocks (relative to baseline) after one, three, and five years on the U.S. current account and the dollar's real (CPI-adjusted) exchange rate against industrial-country currencies. (The simulations were actually run over the period 1986–90.) For the current account we present both the nine-model average and the range.

The MCM's current-account responses are considerably above the average for the U.S. fiscal shock, about equal to the average for the foreign fiscal shock, and somewhat below average for the exchange rate

9. The nine models included in the averages presented in table 2-16 are: DRI, EEC, COMPACT, LINK, LIVERPOOL, IMF-MINIMOD, MCM, McKibbin-Sachs Global Model (MSG), OECD Interlink, and TAYLOR model. Several other models were excluded from the average either because they were unable to run the simulations correctly or because they were obvious outliers.

Table 2-16. *Current-Account and Exchange Rate Effects of Fiscal Shocks and Nominal Dollar Depreciation: Multicountry Model Simulation Results*[a]

Billions of dollars unless otherwise indicated

Number of years after onset of shock	Impact on U.S. current account			Impact on real dollar exchange rate (percent)	
		Nine models			
	MCM	Average	Range	MCM	Nine-model average
U.S. fiscal contraction[b]					
1	10	8	2–19	−1.6	−1.5
3	23	14	6–28	−3.5	−2.0
5	41	20	5–47	−4.6	−2.5
Fiscal expansion in rest of OECD[c]					
1	6	8	2–23	−0.7	−1.1
3	8	8	3–17	0.0	−1.1
5	6	8	1–28	0.2	−1.4
Exogenous nominal depreciation of the dollar[d]					
1	0	4	−15–41	−5	−6
3	12	20	−3–59	−19	−18
5	25	30	7–77	−20	−15

a. Average from simulations run over the period 1986–90 for March 1986 Brookings conference on Empirical Macroeconomics for Interdependent Economies: Where Do We Stand? Reported in Ralph C. Bryant and others, *Empirical Macroeconomics for Interdependent Economies* (Brookings, forthcoming).

b. Sustained cut in government spending equal to 1 percent of GNP.

c. Sustained increase in government spending equal to 1 percent of GNP.

d. Twenty-five percent fall in the dollar against a multilateral trade-weighted average of industrial-country currencies over three years.

shocks. The U.S. fiscal contraction generally has a larger effect than the foreign fiscal expansion on both the current account and the dollar's exchange rate. (The dollar does depreciate in both cases.) The current-account effect grows over time in the case of the U.S. shock, unlike the foreign shock. This can be attributed in part to the greater exchange rate change (which has lagged effects) in the U.S. case, and in part to differences in the impact of the shocks on net investment income.

These results can be explained in turn as follows. The fiscal shocks were run with monetary policy (that is, money growth) held unchanged. Most models (including the MCM) showed significantly larger declines in U.S. real interest rates in response to the U.S. fiscal contraction than increases in foreign real interest rates in response to the foreign fiscal expansion. (In the MCM, at least, this can be attributed in part to differences in money-demand parameters across countries.) The greater interest rate change in the U.S. case produced both a greater real

Table 2-17. *Analysis of Contribution to U.S. Current Account and Dollar Exchange Rate of U.S. and Foreign Fiscal Policies and Additional Dollar Appreciation, 1980–86*

	Change	
Item	*1986 U.S. current account (billions of dollars)*	*Dollar exchange rate (percent)*
U.S. fiscal expansion in 1980–85	− 70[a]	10.5[b]
Foreign fiscal contraction in 1980–85	− 25[c]	0.0[d]
Combined net effect	− 95	10.5
Additional dollar appreciation in 1980–85[e]	− 40	. . .
Memorandum		
Total change in U.S. current account, 1980–86	− 143	. . .

Source: Authors' calculations.

a. U.S. fiscal expansion equal to 3.5 percent of GNP; effect of each 1 percent is to worsen U.S. current account by $20 billion.

b. U.S. fiscal expansion equal to 3.5 percent of GNP; effect of each 1 percent is a 3 percent dollar appreciation.

c. Foreign fiscal contraction equal to 2.5 percent of GNP; effect of each 1 percent is to worsen U.S. current account by $10 billion.

d. Foreign fiscal contraction equal to 2.5 percent of GNP has no effect on dollar exchange rate.

e. Total 1980–85 CPI-adjusted dollar appreciation against G-10 currencies, weighted using multilateral trade shares, was 56 percent; total appreciation against G-10 and eight LDC currencies, weighted using multilateral trade shares, was 48 percent. "Additional" refers to that part of the total 48–56 percent dollar appreciation that is not attributed to shifts in fiscal policy according to the models.

exchange rate change and a greater reduction in U.S. net investment income payments.

Using the simulation results in table 2-16, we present in table 2-17 a rough calculation of the contribution of the 1980–85 fiscal policy shifts. Based on the simulation results, we have chosen to estimate the U.S. current-account effects of U.S. and foreign fiscal shocks (equal to 1 percent of GNP) to be $20 billion and $10 billion, respectively. We accept the asymmetry between current-account effects of the U.S. and foreign fiscal shocks, partly because the U.S. fiscal shock directly affects all U.S. imports, whereas the foreign fiscal shock directly affects only about two-thirds of a noticeably smaller volume of U.S. exports (with exports to developing countries not being directly affected). Also, the U.S. shock appears to have a greater impact through greater exchange rate changes than the foreign shock. We assume, based on a combination of the MCM and average results in table 2-16, that the U.S. shock results in a 3 percent real dollar appreciation, while the foreign shock has only a negligible impact.

Since the Brookings model-comparison exercise documented by Ralph Bryant and others showed the model-simulation results to be relatively linear and symmetrical, we can apply these estimates to the actual fiscal policy changes presented in table 2-15.[10] The calculations in table 2-17 are straightforward. A U.S. fiscal expansion equal to 3.5 percent of GNP results in a $70 billion reduction in the current account. Part of this reduction can be attributed to a 10.5 percent real appreciation of the dollar associated with the fiscal shocks. The foreign fiscal contraction contributed another $25 billion to the deficit, none of which was associated with dollar appreciation. On this basis, fiscal policy shifts accounted for nearly two-thirds of the decline in the U.S. current account, but only about one-fifth of the dollar's real appreciation.

As indicated in figure 2-12, much of the longer-term movement in the CPI-adjusted dollar against the currencies of other major industrial countries over the past decade has been fairly closely associated with swings in the difference between U.S. and other industrial-country long-term real interest rates. Based on MCM simulations, less than half the rise in the real interest differential between 1979 and 1982 can be attributed to fiscal policy shifts.[11] In addition, the dollar appreciated substantially in 1984 and early 1985 even as the interest differential (and the current account) was falling. In brief, the rise in the dollar must be largely attributable to other factors.

Much of the rise in U.S. real interest rates and the interest rate differential in the early 1980s probably can be attributed to the relative tightening of U.S. monetary policy following the shift in monetary policy operating procedures late in 1979. If the rise in the interest differential accounts for two-thirds of the rise in the dollar and if all of the rise in the interest differential not explained by fiscal policy is attributable to U.S. monetary policy, the monetary tightening could account for between one-third and one-half of the total rise in the dollar. The additional rise in the dollar during 1984 over and above that which can be explained by the interest differential must be attributable to other factors. Given that economic fundamentals (real interest rates and the current account) were moving in the "wrong" direction in 1984, some analysts have

10. Ralph C. Bryant and others, eds., *Empirical Macroeconomics for Interdependent Economies* (Brookings, forthcoming).

11. Peter Hooper, "International Repercussions of the U.S. Budget Deficit," International Finance Discussion Paper 246 (Board of Governors of the Federal Reserve System, September 1984).

Figure 2-12. *Real Dollar Exchange Rate and Real Interest Rate Differential, 1974–86*

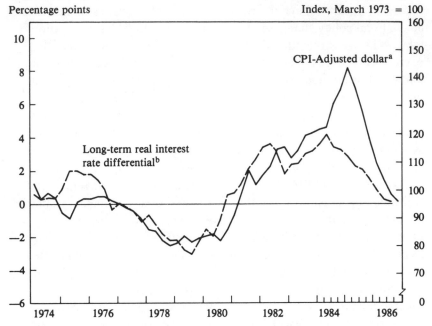

Percentage points   Index, March 1973 = 100

a. All data are quarterly averages. The price-adjusted dollar is the Federal Reserve Board's weighted average index of the exchange value of the dollar against the currencies of the foreign Group-of-Ten countries plus Switzerland, where nominal exchange rates are multiplied by relative levels of consumer price indexes. Weights are proportional to each foreign country's share in world exports plus imports during 1972–76.

b. Long-term real U.S. interest rate minus weighted average of long-term real foreign country interest rates, based on weights described in note a. The long-term real interest rate for each country is a government bond yield on nearest equivalent minus an assumed measure of inflation expectations constructed as a twelve-quarter centered moving average of changes in the country's consumer price index.

described the dollar's continuing rise during that period as a speculative bubble.[12]

In the Brookings model-comparison exercise, an average of the simulation results suggested that a shift in U.S. money growth would significantly affect real interest rates but would have only a negligible impact on the current account. In the case of a monetary tightening, for example, higher interest rates would lead to a higher dollar and lower GNP, which would have offsetting effects on the current account. In rough terms, it appears that the combination of shifts in fiscal policy and a U.S. monetary tightening can explain two-thirds of the fall in the

12. See, for example, Jeffrey A. Frankel and Kenneth Froot, "The Dollar as a Speculative Bubble: A Tale of Fundamentalists and Chartists," Working Paper 1854 (Cambridge, Mass.: National Bureau of Economic Research, March 1986).

current account and most of the rise in the real interest differential. Much of the rest of the fall in the current account can probably be attributed to the additional rise in the dollar that may well have been due to bubbles or other exchange market dynamics.

Recent Changes in U.S. Price Competitiveness

Given the importance of the decline in U.S. price competitiveness during the early 1980s to the growth of the U.S. deficit, any significant reversal of the deficit will require a significant recovery of U.S. price competitiveness. By some measures, the dollar declined substantially between early 1985 and mid-1987, but it had not yet had major visible effects on the U.S. trade balance in nominal terms, although the trade balance in real terms had begun to show some improvement in the first half of 1987.

Several explanations for the slow response of the deficit minimize the apparent gain in U.S. price competitiveness. One explanation is that the Federal Reserve Board staff's exchange rate index, which includes only the currencies of the Group-of-Ten countries, gives a misleading picture of movements in the dollar. Other indexes, such as one recently constructed by the Federal Reserve Bank of Dallas that includes a number of developing-country currencies, show little decline in the dollar. However, the Dallas index is significantly biased by the inclusion of exchange rates in nominal terms for a number of high-inflation Latin American countries. Figure 2-13 shows several indexes in real terms (all adjusted for relative consumer prices), including: the Group-of-Ten index; an index for eight major developing countries, Mexico, Brazil, Korea, Taiwan, Hong Kong, Singapore, Malaysia, and the Philippines; and an index combining the other two using 1978–83 world trade weights. Although the dollar continued to appreciate in real terms against the eight developing-country currencies through much of 1986, it had still reversed about two-thirds of its earlier rise against the total basket of eighteen currencies by the end of 1986. When the index is constructed using bilateral U.S. nonoil import shares as weights (figure 2-14), the dollar fell less, but it still reversed more than half of its earlier rise. Given the importance of German and Japanese competition with the United States in third markets, the multilateral index probably best indicates

Figure 2-13. *Alternative Indexes of the CPI-Adjusted Dollar Exchange Rate, Weighted by Multilateral Trade Shares, 1973–86*

Index, 1973:1 = 100

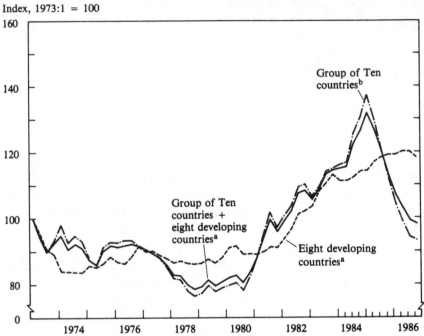

a. Developing countries included are Mexico, Brazil, Hong Kong, Malaysia, Philippines, Singapore, South Korea, and Taiwan.
b. Includes Switzerland in addition to foreign G-10 countries.

the price competitiveness of U.S. exports, whereas the bilateral (import-weighted) index is probably more important to understanding the behavior of nonoil import prices.

A second possible reason for the slow response of the deficit to the dollar's decline is that the strong trend growth in Japanese labor productivity in manufacturing may have been significantly offsetting the effects of the dollar's fall against the yen in nominal terms.[13] However, data on comparative manufacturing unit labor costs in dollars, shown in table 2-18, do not suggest such offsetting effects. Indeed, even expressed in terms of local currencies, Japanese unit labor costs rose relative to U.S. unit labor costs after early 1985. Thus the fall in the dollar was more

13. Richard C. Marston, "Real Exchange Rates and Productivity Growth in the United States and Japan," Working Paper 1922 (Cambridge, Mass.: National Bureau of Economic Research, May 1986).

Figure 2-14. *Alternative Indexes of the CPI-Adjusted Dollar Exchange Rate, Weighted by Bilateral U.S. Nonoil Imports Shares, 1973–86*

Index, 1973:1 = 100

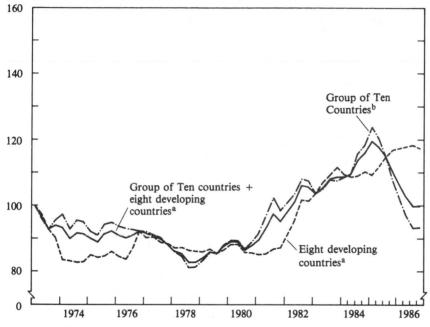

a. Developing countries included are Mexico, Brazil, Hong Kong, Malaysia, Philippines, Singapore, South Korea, and Taiwan.
b. Includes Switzerland in addition to foreign G-10 countries.

than fully reflected in a gain in U.S. competitiveness in terms of relative unit labor costs in dollars. (For further discussion of this argument, see chapter 4.)

Finally, it has been suggested that foreign exporters, after having increased their profit margins significantly during the dollar's rise, had ample room to cut their margins during the dollar's fall. Catherine Mann provides empirical evidence to support this hypothesis using U.S. import price data and proxies for foreign cost data.[14] Transitory behavior of this type is also evident in the estimated aggregate nonoil import price equation already discussed. Different theoretical bases for such behavior can be found in Mann and in a paper by Richard Baldwin and Paul

14. Catherine L. Mann, "Prices, Profit Margins, and Exchange Rates," *Federal Reserve Bulletin*, vol. 72 (June 1986), pp. 366–79.

Table 2-18. *U.S., German, and Japanese Unit Labor Costs, Selected Periods, 1980:2–1986:2*

Country	Logarithmic percentage change	
	1980:2–1985:1	1985:1–1986:2
United States	11.0	−0.2
Germany		
Dollars	− 50.9	40.0
Local currency	7.8	2.8
Japan		
Dollars	− 2.0	35.4[a]
Local currency	8.7	3.6[a]
Ratio, United States to Germany	62.0	− 40.2
Ratio, United States to Japan	13.0	− 35.6[a]

Sources: For Japan and Germany, see OECD, *Main Economic Indicators* (Paris: OECD), July 1982, pp. 90, 122, and April 1987, pp. 94, 122; for the United States, see Bureau of Labor Statistics, *Monthly Labor Review*, vol. 104 (October 1981), p. 92, and vol. 110 (February 1987), p. 85.
a. Through 1986:1 for Japan.

Krugman.[15] The latter study suggests that significant fixed costs to market entry may lead export firms to stay in the market longer and cut their profit margins more in the face of a home-currency appreciation than they would if entry costs were not significant.

Data on comparative U.S., German, and Japanese export prices published by the Bureau of Labor Statistics provide a mixed picture, however. U.S. price competitiveness vis-à-vis Germany and Japan is of particular importance, partly because these two countries represent the major export competitors in world markets for U.S. manufactured goods, partly because the two ran a combined current-account surplus of $122 billion in 1986 (compared with the U.S. deficit of $145 billion), and partly because it is against the currencies of these two countries that the dollar has fallen most noticeably since early 1985. Any significant decline in the U.S. deficit is likely to be reflected in a decline in Japanese and German surpluses.

Table 2-19 presents changes in the ratios of U.S. export prices to German and Japanese export prices for various aggregate commodity categories over the periods before and after the dollar's peak in March 1985.

The price data underlying the ratio changes shown in the table were

15. Mann, "Prices, Profit Margins, and Exchange Rates"; Richard E. Baldwin and Paul R. Krugman, "Persistent Trade Effects of Large Exchange Rate Shocks," Working Paper 2017 (Cambridge, Mass.: National Bureau of Economic Research, August 1986).

Table 2-19. *Changes in Export Price Competitiveness of the United States vis-à-vis Japan and Germany, Selected Periods, June 1980–June 1986*[a]

| | Logarithmic percentage change[b] | |
| | June 1980– | March 1985– |
Item	March 1985	June 1986
Ratio of yen to dollar		
Nominal rate	17	−43
CPI-adjusted rate	29	−42
WPI-adjusted rate	34	−36
Ratio of U.S. export prices to Japanese export prices		
All products (1.0)	26	−20
Chemicals (.07)	6	−3
Metal products (.18)	24	−6
General machinery (.21)	27	−29
Electrical machinery (.19)	25	−16
Transport equipment (.24)	26	−27
Miscellaneous manufactured goods (.08)	25	−19
Household electrical equipment (.10)	15	−15
Integrated circuits (.01)	72	−16
Ratio of deutsche mark to dollar		
Nominal rate	62	−39
CPI-adjusted rate	69	−36
WPI-adjusted rate	60	−37
Ratio of U.S. export prices to German export prices		
All products (1.0)	60	−36
Chemicals (.13)	44	−36
Machinery transport (.44)	69	−39
Other manufactured goods (.32)	59	−35

Sources: Exchange rates: FRB; export prices: BLS.
a. A positive number indicates an increase in U.S. relative prices or a decline in U.S. price competitiveness. Numbers in parentheses are weights in total indexes (based on 1980 Japanese and German export shares).
b. The logarithmic percentage change (for example, in variable X) is calculated as $100 \cdot \Delta \log X$. This measure of change has the advantage of showing quantitatively symmetrical changes for both increases and decreases.

obtained from national sources, based on surveys of actual transactions prices adjusted for shifts in quality. The overall U.S.-German and U.S.-Japanese ratios were aggregated from ratios for narrowly defined commodity categories using 1980 German and Japanese export shares, respectively.

The data in tables 2-18 and 2-19 suggest that movements in U.S.-German export prices in dollars followed very closely both the change in the deutsche mark–dollar exchange rate and movements in U.S.-German unit labor costs in dollars. In brief, there is little evidence to suggest significant shifts in profit margins by German exporters. In the Japanese case, however, evidence of a shift in profit margins is apparent. The ratio of U.S. to Japanese export prices fell noticeably less than either the yen-dollar exchange rate or the ratio of U.S. to Japanese unit labor costs in dollars. In both the German and Japanese cases, however, substantial gains in U.S. export price competitiveness occurred during 1985–86. To the extent that price competitiveness is an important factor in determining trade flows, U.S. exports could be expected to regain some of their recent losses in world market shares during 1986–87 and beyond.

These shifts in relative export prices may not have been fully reflected in the relative price of U.S. imports. Between the first quarter of 1985 and the fourth quarter of 1986, U.S. nonoil import prices (based on Bureau of Labor Statistics data) rose about 12 percent. The prices of imports from Canada and developing countries, against whose currencies the dollar has not changed appreciably, would have tended to hold down the total import price increase. It is also conceivable that German and Japanese exporters have been less inclined to raise their dollar export prices in the U.S. market than they have in other markets.

CHAPTER THREE

The U.S. External Deficit: Diagnosis, Prognosis, and Cure

RALPH C. BRYANT AND GERALD HOLTHAM

FOR MOST of the 1980s the current-account deficit in the U.S. balance of payments was just an economic statistic confined to the business pages of newspapers. Since mid-1986, however, that external deficit has become a central economic and political issue. Monthly trade statistics now generate front-page headlines. The new public interest is justified. Because of the deterioration in the external deficit since 1980, the United States has slipped—suddenly and dramatically—from being the world's largest creditor country to being the world's largest debtor. An external deficit as large as the existing one—some $140 billion in 1986—is very difficult to remove quickly. Fears that U.S. indebtedness will continue to grow, perhaps to an alarming extent, are well founded.

Unfortunately, increased interest in the external deficit has not led to an increase in clear thinking about it. In the United States, ill-informed commentators assert that recent depreciations of the dollar are failing to reduce the external deficit. Protectionist sentiment is intense, even though the deficit was not caused by growing protectionism abroad and will not be cured by it at home. Facile critics in other countries call on the United States to "put its house in order"—always good advice, especially applied to someone else's house—with no apparent awareness of the likely consequences if the advice were followed. Some foreign governments seem to believe that a further depreciation of the U.S. dollar would be bad for them, but a recession in the United States would be a matter of indifference. In either event, they are reluctant to assume public responsibility for the level of demand in their economies.

In this chapter, informed by the analyses presented at the January 1987 workshop at the Brookings Institution, we give our conclusions about the causes of the U.S. external deficit, its probable future evolution, and the best means to reduce it.

57

As Helkie and Hooper's analysis in chapter 2 suggests, the causes of the swelling of the U.S. external deficit in the past six years are chiefly macroeconomic. Given the path followed by the dollar's exchange value and the course of domestic demand growth in the United States and major foreign countries, there is no mystery about the recent history. Moreover, the evolution of domestic demands and the dollar's exchange value were themselves largely a consequence of macroeconomic policies here and abroad (though the dollar's final surge in 1984–85 is inexplicable except in terms of speculation and exchange market dynamics). The largest part of the external deficit is attributable to these policies, not to increased foreign protectionism or to structural changes in the U.S. and foreign economies.

The fall of the dollar between the first quarter of 1985 and the spring of 1987 will probably result, other things being equal, in a moderate improvement in the external balance during 1987 and a larger improvement in 1988. On its own, however, that dollar depreciation is unlikely to hold the deficit substantially below $100 billion. Without changes in governments' policies or a further dollar depreciation, the U.S. current account is likely to deteriorate anew after 1989, in part because of growing net interest payments to foreigners on the growing external debt. A further substantial fall of the dollar would make the deficit somewhat worse in 1987, but would improve it after 1988. However if present policies remained unchanged, a further large depreciation would threaten renewed inflation in the United States and recession abroad.

An appropriate reduction of the external deficit during the next few years would withdraw at least $100 billion from economic activity in the rest of the world. Whether such a reduction were achieved by dollar depreciation or by reduced activity in the U.S. economy, it would have a contractionary effect abroad. Unless offset by policy actions by foreign governments, the contractionary impetus would be dangerous at a time of expected slow growth and an incipient debt crisis.

The world economic situation thus cries out for cooperative macro-economic policies. The most important elements of an international agreement would be joint commitment to the goal of shrinking the U.S. external deficit and the counterpart surpluses of other industrial countries; credible commitments by foreign governments to strengthen domestic demand as export demand is withdrawn; a credible commitment by the United States to change the mix of its policies, ensuring a reduction in its structural budget deficit; and a "cooperative presumption'' that an orderly further depreciation of the dollar would support the other agreed goals and policies. The agreement should also reemphasize the need to avoid additional protectionist measures.

The February 1987 meeting of finance ministers of the six largest industrialized countries and the June 1987 summit meeting among leaders of seven major industrialized countries produced hesitant gestures in some of these directions. Unless there were hidden agreements, however, the outcomes fell far short of requirements. And the commitment (if such it was) to maintain the dollar at current parities had the potential to be mainly counterproductive.

What Caused the Ballooning of the External Deficit?

To understand why the external deficit grew so large, it is helpful to distinguish proximate causes from more fundamental ones. By proximate causes we mean, for example, the growth rates of output in the United States and abroad, rates of capacity utilization, and the course of exchange rates. All of these variables influence imports and exports and hence the external balance. But they are all themselves determined within the world economic system by more fundamental factors, for example, the policies of governments or weather-induced changes in world agricultural harvests.

Given the way the proximate determinants of the current account turned out, past macroeconomic relationships can successfully predict the deterioration of the U.S. external imbalance. This point is clearly illustrated in Annex figure I-2. The six macroeconometric models participating in the Brookings workshop (identified earlier in the Introduction to this volume) were asked to "predict" the external deficit for 1980–86 by running their equations for the volumes and prices of exports and imports. All of the models took as given the historical values for exchange rates, domestic producer prices, and economic activity in the United States and other countries. As figure I-2 shows, each model predicted current-account deficits very close to the actual values. The predictions were often within a few billion dollars of the actual deficit in 1986, more than five years after the start of the dynamic simulations.

The consensus displayed in figure I-2 is comforting but, of course, does not necessarily mean that economic behavior is well understood; the successful predictions could be attributable to offsetting errors. For example, a model could predict the trade balance correctly by predicting imports and exports equally wrongly with the errors in the same direction. Alternatively, the value of exports or imports could be correctly predicted but only because big surprises in the volume of trade were offset by big surprises in the opposite direction in trade prices. Several of the models participating in the Brookings workshop do display offsetting errors of that sort so that, for example, their predictions of components of the trade balance have percentage errors that are large in relation to the errors on the trade balance itself. Economists' ability to forecast detailed patterns of trade is limited. However, the various models made their larger mistakes over different components of the current-account balance. There were few common surprises. Furthermore, the more successful models showed no sign of errors growing over time. They were as likely to make a sizable mistake for 1980 as for 1985. That fact is strong evidence against the assertion that there has been a break in historical relationships. Such a break would lead to sustained or cumulating prediction errors.

What were the chief movements in the components of the external deficit associated with its growth in 1980–86? As Helkie and Hooper point out, the deterioration cannot be blamed on price changes; in particular, the dollar prices of nonagricultural exports and nonoil imports showed relatively little net change over 1980–86. Rises in foreign currency prices were offset by the dollar's appreciation. Rather, the swelling deficit stemmed from a doubling in the quantity of nonoil imports while U.S. manufactured exports stagnated and agricultural exports fell sharply. The fall in oil prices, combined with energy conservation efforts, led to a sharp drop in the value of oil imports. These movements in the components of the trade balance combined to produce the 1980–86 deterioration of $127 billion. A further deterioration of $20 billion occurred in the nontrade components of the current account.

The developments in nonagricultural exports and nonoil imports were captured very broadly by the econometric models in the Brookings workshop. The one development that was substantially missed was the extent of the slump in agricultural exports, especially in 1985 and 1986. It seems to exceed what can be ascribed to relative prices alone and may reflect structural changes, notably the reduction of U.S. price supports for agriculture and the third world's debt crisis, which reduced the ability of many developing countries to import American food. While total U.S. exports to industrialized countries have grown, if modestly, since 1980, those to the developing countries have fallen, especially those to Latin America.

It has often been asserted that the pricing practices of foreign exporters to the United States were unusual during the 1980–86 swings in the dollar. It is true that dollar prices of imports were not reduced fully in proportion as the currency appreciated, and they have not been increased fully during its decline. Foreign exporters have been taking some of the recent strain on their profit margins (see chapter 2). This behavior, however, is not unusual. Most of the models predicted something like it as the normal response to currency fluctuations. There is some evidence of unusually large prediction errors for import prices during the second half of 1986, which may indicate a recent change in the pricing policies of foreign exporters. So far, though, that evidence is not substantial enough to make us reject the import-price relationships embedded in the more successful models.

Among the proximate factors used by models to explain the external deficit, two are overwhelmingly important: strong U.S. domestic demand growth during a world recession and a relatively feeble recovery abroad, and the large appreciation of the dollar from 1980 through early 1985. An additional factor that seems to be important, but not adequately captured by the models, is the debt crisis and persistent weakness of activity in developing countries, which were important U.S. markets.

The existence of several factors all working in the same direction, tending to widen the deficit, means paradoxically that the deficit is too easy to explain. The deterioration can be accounted for in different ways by giving different weights to the various factors.

For example, Helkie and Hooper report that the Multicountry Model (MCM) of the Federal Reserve Board staff suggests that if U.S. and foreign GNPs had remained at their 1980 levels, all other things being equal, about a fourth of the deterioration in the U.S. external deficit (measured in constant prices) would not have occurred. If relative prices in the United States and abroad had remained at their 1980 levels, about three-fourths of the constant-price deficit would not have occurred (see chapter 2, table 2-12).

Other models give a somewhat different breakdown. The model of the Japanese government's Economic Planning Agency gives much more importance to relative growth rates, leaving less than two-thirds of the deficit to be explained by competitiveness (primarily exchange rate) effects. The models of Data Resources Inc. and the National

Institute of Economic and Social Research in London give slightly more relative weight to dollar appreciation than does the MCM. These differences have more than historical significance. They mean that, even on the basis of common assumptions, the models predict a different future evolution of the deficit.

Economists are less secure when analyzing the fundamentals that drive the proximate determinants of the external deficit. Growth differentials between the United States and other OECD countries are substantially explicable by policy differences, particularly relative fiscal policies, which were expansionary in the United States after 1981 and equally contractionary elsewhere. On the basis of actual fiscal and monetary policies, however, the full models from which the current-account sectors were extracted on average would have predicted only a half or less of the actual rise in the dollar. No empirical economic model can successfully explain the remaining appreciation, particularly not the surge in 1984 and the first months of 1985. That failure means in turn that the models are capable of predicting only half to two-thirds of the external deficit on the basis of policies alone. The failure to predict more is essentially a failure to predict exchange rates.

The inadequacy of models in predicting exchange rates could be interpreted as evidence that the models will understate the effectiveness of macroeconomic policies in reducing the deficit because they will understate the policies' exchange rate effects. That inference is not robust, however, if other factors independent of policy (for example, volatile shifts in private sector expectations) significantly determined exchange rates during the early 1980s and could similarly drive them in the future.

Why Has the External Deficit Remained Large?

By the first quarter of 1987, more than two years after the pendulum of exchange rates had begun to swing sharply down again, the U.S. external deficit persisted at unprecedented levels. That fact occasioned a good deal of comment. It was frequently asserted, for example, that adjustment was taking "longer than expected."

Is there really a puzzle about what has been happening? Helkie and Hooper address that question at the end of their analysis. Both their conclusion and our own answer, drawing on the workshop findings, are no. Expectations that the improvement would take less time were based largely on incomplete or faulty analysis.[1]

It is sometimes asserted that the dollar has not really declined much when account is taken of two factors: the exchange values of many of the currencies of important newly industrializing countries (a number of which are pegged to the dollar), and relative price and productivity trends here and abroad. In fact, the dollar has depreciated substantially from its 1985 peak against a trade-weighted index of foreign currencies. This conclusion holds even when the weights in the index reflect the bilateral trade of the United States with other countries (rather than more comprehensive measures of countries' multilateral trade) and even when the currencies of developing-country trading partners are included in the index. Moreover, the depreciation is substantial in inflation-adjusted terms (see chapter 2, particularly figure 2-14).[2]

The effective depreciation of the dollar relevant to its effects on the current-account balance is, to be sure, less than proportionate to the dollar's steep decline since the short-lived peak of February–March 1985. That peak was not sustained very long and was never incorporated in trade prices. And while the dollar fell throughout the last three quarters of 1985, its average effective value during 1985 was still well above its average value during 1984. Period averages are more important than day-to-day quotations in assessing the influence of exchange rates on trade prices.

When the path of the dollar's exchange value is correctly incorporated into the analysis, the time taken for the external deficit to begin improving is not a surprise. Historical relationships make it clear that a lengthy period is necessary. First, trade prices respond sluggishly to exchange

1. A word of caution is in order about the monthly trade figures that have been the object of so much attention. These data are notoriously erratic and typically subject to substantial revision. It takes a sequence of monthly statistics before any trend can be reliably detected.

2. For the United States, exchange rate indexes calculated with bilateral trade weights fluctuate less than indexes based on multilateral trade weights, and indexes that include developing countries' currencies tend to fluctuate less than indexes excluding those currencies. Many alternative measures of weighted-average exchange rates may be calculated. Each has advantages and limitations, and no single average is preferable for all analytical purposes. It is misleading to emphasize a *nominal* index that includes the currencies of high-inflation countries (for example, Brazil and Mexico); when high-inflation countries are included in an index, one should focus on the inflation-adjusted version.

rate movements; this lag is especially important for the dollar prices of U.S. imports. Second, the volumes of exports and imports (flows at constant prices) react slowly to changes in relative prices; distributed lags extending beyond two years are common in trade models. Third, though both react slowly, trade prices adjust faster than trade volumes, leading in the short run to "*J*-curve" effects in the current-price balances. (In particular, import volumes initially decline less in response to dollar depreciation than import prices rise, leading initially to an increase rather than a fall in the value of imports.) Even though the trade and current-account balances initially fail to improve at current prices, a gradual improvement in the constant-price balances does begin immediately. Given the nearly continuous depreciation of the dollar over the two years following the 1985 peak, moreover, an entire family of *J* curves has been in effect. The deficit must navigate around the whole family of curves before the full effects of the exchange rate changes become evident.

Other countries have typically waited two years or more to see the benefits of a currency depreciation. In addition, adjustment of the U.S. external deficit in response to currency depreciation is probably slower than it would be for other countries. The U.S. domestic market is the world's largest and most important. It is likely that foreign exporters take account of U.S. domestic prices and set their own prices competitively, rather than applying a fixed markup on their costs. In other words, in their effort to keep a position in the U.S. market, foreign suppliers accept more variable profit margins than they do elsewhere and more than U.S. suppliers accept when exporting. Such pricing behavior is not a surprise; several models predict it. It does not negate the effects of exchange rate changes on trade, but it does slow down speeds of adjustment.[3] Eventually import prices come to reflect foreign costs, or the supply of foreign goods falls back, reflecting the lower profit margins in the U.S. market and a consequent reduced investment in marketing imports. This latter effect, however, could take years to reveal itself fully.[4]

3. Helkie and Hooper note in chapter 2 that there is some evidence that pricing lags may have lengthened in recent years.

4. For a detailed analysis of the obstinate trade deficit, see Paul R. Krugman and Richard E. Baldwin, "The Persistence of the U.S. Trade Deficit," *Brookings Papers on Economic Activity, 1:1987,* pp. 1–43.

Will the External Deficit Ever Decline?

If there is little or no mystery about the recent history, what lies ahead for the U.S. external deficit? Consider first the prospects in the shorter run, through the end of 1988.

The modeling groups in the Brookings workshop were asked to project the external deficit and its components, at both constant and current prices, assuming that the U.S. and foreign economies each grew at similar rates and that the exchange value of the dollar remained unchanged in real terms from the average value prevailing in the third quarter of 1986.

Using those assumptions, the models differ considerably in their projections of the external deficit. The greatest variation stems from different estimates of the consequences of dollar depreciation. Nonetheless, the models agree in predicting a big improvement in the constant-price deficit (real net exports of goods and services) during 1987–88.

Between the third quarter of 1986 and the second quarter of 1987, the dollar declined by another 7 to 10 percent (the amount varying with the type of index used). The likely effects of that additional depreciation can be roughly calculated using other materials from the modeling groups presented at the workshop. Figure 3-1 shows the actual history of constant-price net exports of goods and services through 1986 and projections from the various models for 1987–91, adjusted for an additional 10 percent depreciation. Figure 3-2 shows a comparable series for the current-account balance at current prices.

Further information about these conditional projections is given in the illustrative calculations in table 3-1, where we use a weighted average of the projections of the models and of the effects they simulate for an additional 10 percent depreciation of the dollar. We show a rough "combined-model" projection for both constant-price net exports of goods and services and the current-account balance in current dollars. The weights used to derive the combined-model projections are based on the relative performance of the models in predicting the 1980–86 history. For the external deficit at current prices, the combined-model projection shows an improvement of some $30 billion to $35 billion over 1987–88, although most of it comes in 1988. The additional dollar depreciation that occurred between the fall of 1986 and late January 1987

Figure 3-1. *Real Net Exports of U.S. Goods and Services,*
Actual 1979–86 and Conditional Projections 1987–91

Billions of constant 1982 dollars

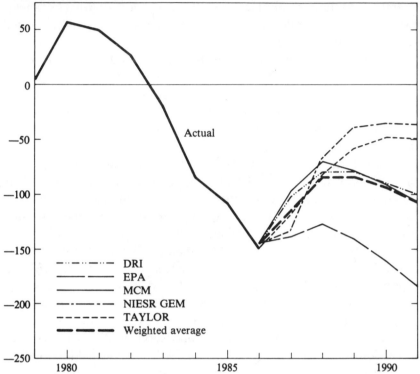

does not help in the shortest run, adding another "*J* curve" to those
already operating from the earlier depreciations. The trade deficit
improves by $10 billion to $15 billion in 1987 and $20 billion to $30 billion
in 1988. Net exports of goods and services at constant 1982 prices
improve by as much as $30 billion to $35 billion in 1987 and by the same
amount again in 1988. It is the deficit in current prices that gets the lion's
share of public attention. The current-price balance does show what the
United States must borrow abroad to finance the deficit. Yet it is the
deficit in constant prices that is relevant for assessing influences on real
GNP and jobs, both in the U.S. economy and abroad. For 1987–88,
moreover, the reduction in the constant-price deficit is significantly
larger than the improvement measured in current prices. (We come back
to this point below.)

Unfortunately, prospects for improvement are not so rosy beyond

Figure 3-2. *U.S. Current-Account Balance, Actual 1979–86 and Conditional Projections 1987–91*

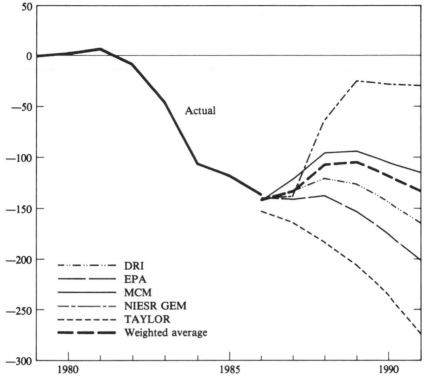

Billions of current dollars

Legend:
- DRI
- EPA
- MCM
- NIESR GEM
- TAYLOR
- Weighted average

1988. The models differ considerably in their projections of the deficit for 1989–91 (see figures 3-1 and 3-2). The greatest variation stems from different estimates of the consequences of dollar depreciation. Still, there is a consensus that the depreciation that occurred through mid-1987 will not be sufficient to eradicate the deficit at either current or constant prices. If there were no further dollar depreciation from the spring 1987 level, and if the economies of the United States and the rest of the world were to grow at roughly similar rates, the lagged effects of the currency changes occurring through spring 1987 would have largely worked themselves out by 1989. Indeed, the projections show the trade and current-account balances deteriorating again after 1989. A deterioration can also be seen, though less prominently, in the constant-price projections. As a percentage of GNP, the current-account deficit never

Table 3-1. *Projections of the External U.S. Deficit, 1986–91*[a]

Deficit component	1986[b]	1987[b]	1988	1989	1990	1991
	Billions of constant 1982 U.S. dollars					
Real net exports of goods and services						
Original projection[c]	−146	−120	−107	−116	−132	−147
Estimated effects of additional						
10 percent dollar depreciation[d]	. . .	7	28	41	48	52
Adjusted projection	−146	−113	−79	−75	−84	−95
	Billions of current U.S. dollars					
Current-account balance						
Original projection[c]	−142	−134	−122	−132	−150	−170
Estimated effects of additional						
10 percent dollar depreciation[d]	. . .	−1	13	24	28	33
Adjusted projection	−142	−135	−109	−108	−122	−137
Memorandum: Estimated effects of						
1 percent slower growth abroad	. . .	−2	−8	−17	−28	−42
Merchandise trade balance[e]						
Original projection[c]	−147	−133	−120	−127	−142	−158
Estimated effects of additional						
10 percent dollar depreciation[d]	. . .	−1	11	21	23	26
Adjusted projection	−147	−134	−109	−106	−119	−132

Source: Simulations prepared for January 20, 1987, workshop by participating modeling groups. See text for further discussion.

a. The figures in this table are weighted-average calculations yielding "combined-model" projections. The underlying weights for each model for each variable were the normalized reciprocal of the sum of squared prediction errors recorded by each model for each variable over 1980–85. Weights were calculated for imports and exports (both volumes and values), for trade balances at current prices, and for real net exports at 1982 prices. To simplify the calculations for the purposes of exposition, the different weights were averaged to produce a single overall set of weights used throughout the table. The final model weights were (in percentage of the total): DRI, 19; EPA, 22; NIESR GEM, 19; MCM, 36; TAYLOR, 4. The underlying data were not available for OECD and WHARTON. The weights used here should not be regarded as a guide to model rankings in any general sense. The historical performance of the models was not compared comprehensively for all variables, and the historical tracking experiments used only one set of values for forcing variables over a single sample.

b. For cases where the underlying model projections showed sizable errors for 1986 (because the projections had been prepared without the benefit of actual data for the final months of 1986), the 1986 levels were adjusted to actual data and the resulting adjustment was phased out during 1987.

c. These weighted-average projections are contingent on the set of assumptions used for the workshop. Key assumptions included output growth of 3 percent a year in the United States and Europe, 3.5 percent in Japan; an average inflation rate of 3.5 percent a year in the United States and in the rest of the OECD; and no change in real exchange rates from the averages prevailing in the third quarter of 1986. For further details, see the Annex.

d. These estimates are a weighted average of simulated responses by models to a 10 percent depreciation of the U.S. dollar against the yen and EEC currencies. A 10 percent depreciation of the dollar against all other currencies is estimated to give effects about 50 percent larger. Note that these estimates represent only *partial* effects of exchange depreciation (on traded quantities in the case of real net exports of goods and services, on traded quantities and trade prices for the current balance and trade balance); repercussions through output and domestic inflation are ignored.

e. Trade balance data were not available for the TAYLOR model, so these weighted-average projections were made using only DRI, EPA, NIESR GEM, and MCM.

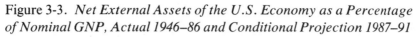

Figure 3-3. *Net External Assets of the U.S. Economy as a Percentage of Nominal GNP, Actual 1946–86 and Conditional Projection 1987–91*

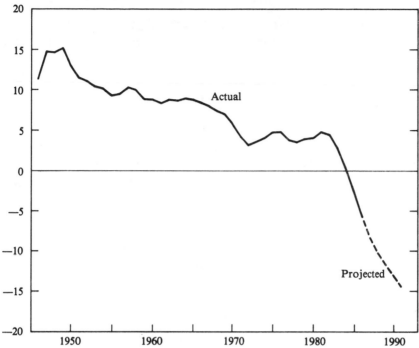

again reaches its 1986 level of about 3⅓ percent, but after falling to a low of around 2 percent in 1989, it rises slightly thereafter.

With the external deficit still fairly large even after 1989, the net external debt position of the United States would still grow rapidly. Correspondingly, debt service payments to foreigners would continue to increase, adding larger and larger negative numbers to the current account. Some idea of the magnitude of the external-debt problem is suggested in figure 3-3, which shows the end-year net external assets of the U.S. economy deflated by the nominal value of U.S. GNP. The data through 1986 are actual history; the figures for 1987–91 are derived from the projected current-account balances shown in table 3-1.

Virtually all analysts expect a continuing deterioration in the net external-asset position and hence a growing burden of debt servicing. The prediction that the current balance will start to worsen again after 1989, therefore, is likely to be robust. The finding that the *trade* balance could worsen after 1989, however, is less secure. Predictions of a worsening trade balance after 1989 are basically the result of relative parameter sizes in the models, particularly the so-called income elasticities of imports and exports.

The rate of growth of U.S. imports with respect to the growth of either U.S. GNP or domestic demand is commonly estimated to be greater than the corresponding rate of growth of U.S. exports with respect to the growth of foreign GNP or domestic demand. The implication of that difference is that the U.S. trade deficit would widen if all parts of the world economy grew at the same rate (all other things, including exchange rates, remaining unchanged). Furthermore, analysts commonly estimate the income elasticities of both imports and exports as greater than unity, which means trade flows tend to grow faster than GNP. Because the United States starts from a position of trade deficit, such estimates mean that balanced growth at home and abroad would lead to a growing deficit, both in absolute terms and as a proportion of GNP.

The estimates of different income elasticities are obtained by statistical regression analysis of recent history. However, the estimation of the elasticities can get mixed up with trends in trade generated by other factors. For example, it has been plausibly argued that American consumers' tastes have become more international in recent decades, leading to a relatively rapid growth of imports. If that internationalization is complete, or if American industry now responds by producing goods with the requisite international flavor, there may be no reason for imports to grow so much faster than income in the future. We regard this issue as an open question and hence would not be inclined to put too much weight on projections of a deterioration in the trade balance after 1989. On the other hand, if the rise in oil prices in late 1986 and early 1987 is maintained or augmented, a rise in the value of oil imports could cause a deterioration in the trade balance. At any rate, it is a matter of concern for policy that the trade deficit could get stuck above $100 billion while the current-account deficit deteriorates in relation to GNP.

A mechanical application of model results might appear to suggest that a further depreciation of the dollar of 20 to 30 percent against all other currencies—not simply the yen and the currencies of the European Monetary System—would be necessary and sufficient to achieve eventual elimination of the U.S. external deficit. That inference, however, would not be justified. The calculations underlying it are partial—the result of changing one variable, such as the dollar's exchange value, while all others are held fixed. In practice such a large additional depreciation would not leave all other variables unchanged. On the contrary, it would have a strong inflationary impact in the United States and a deflationary impact abroad. Both of those effects would tend to feed back on the external balance, thus limiting its improvement. Indeed, if the United States were able to achieve a swing of even $100 billion in its real net exports of goods and services, the domestic economy would probably overheat in the absence of other policy measures.

Moreover, the exchange value of the dollar is not a policy instrument that governments can manipulate at will. When assessing the probable effects of a large dollar depreciation, it is thus necessary to ask what induced the depreciation. If a further 20 to 30 percent decline in the dollar were brought about by market expectations, the effects would be quite different from those that would happen as a result of deliberate monetary policy.

All in all, a safer inference is that while the decline in the dollar from early 1985 to mid-1987 will make a substantial contribution to reducing the external deficit, and while some further depreciation is probably in order, it is highly unlikely that the deficit can be removed by dollar depreciation alone. The conclusion is inescapable that other public policy action is required.[5]

Risks of Recession in the World Economy

The preceding conclusion is strengthened when the prospects for demand and output in the world economy are taken into account. During the years when the U.S. external deficit was worsening, U.S. real GNP grew on average at an annual rate of less than 2½ percent, while total domestic demand at constant prices grew at over 3½ percent. The growing excess of imports over exports was a significant drag on the expansion of the economy. In 1986, when the U.S. economy grew by about 2¼ percent, domestic demand at constant prices grew by over 3

---

5. The goal of "removing" the external deficit should probably be interpreted as reducing the deficit into a range of $15 billion to $35 billion. The *measured* sum of all nations' current-account balances is a large negative number, some $70 billion to $90 billion in the last several years, whereas the sum would be zero if all balances were measured correctly. It is widely believed that at least $20 billion of this global statistical discrepancy represents errors and omissions in the U.S. current-account balance, overstating by that amount the true size of the deficit.

percent; the deterioration in the external balance at constant prices cost about 1 percentage point of growth.

If the external balance at constant prices simply fails to deteriorate in calendar year 1987, and if domestic demand holds up, growth would be 1 percent faster than in 1986. The projections summarized in the third line of table 3-1, moreover, imply a further boost to the 1987 growth rate of nearly 1 percentage point. The total swing in the external balance could therefore add as much as 2 percentage points to the 1987 growth rate. Of course, that figure also depends on particular assumptions about foreign demand growth that might well not be realized.

For the world economy as a whole, faster U.S. growth due to a swing in the external balance is at someone else's expense: in effect, coins are taken out of the left pocket and put into the right. Thus, in sharp contrast to 1983–86, when the growing U.S. current-account deficit supported growth in the rest of the world, correction of the deficit must now subject foreign economies to a strongly contractionary influence.

In Japan, for example, during 1983–86 domestic demand grew by barely 3¼ percent a year, yet real GNP was able to grow at 3¾ percent because of the growing external surplus. (Potential growth in Japan has been estimated at 4 percent by official agencies.) If the real Japanese surplus in 1987 were to decline by a fifth of its 1986 amount, real GNP in Japan would be reduced by nearly 1 percent. If total domestic demand in 1987 grew at only the 1986 rate of about 3¾ percent, real GNP growth would be stuck in the 2¾ percent range, failing to reach 3 percent for the second year in succession.

As of spring 1987, prospects for real growth in Europe and Japan during 1987–88 were already soggy. In December 1986 the OECD Secretariat, for example, forecast real growth in 1987 for OECD countries other than the United States of only 2¾ percent, with 2¾ percent for Japan and 3 percent for Germany. The projected growth for the second half of 1987 and first half of 1988 was slightly weaker than for the first half of 1987. Economic indicators released subsequently suggested that domestic demand was growing more slowly than was expected, particularly in Germany. Furthermore, the dollar had already depreciated by an additional 5 to 8 percent since the OECD and other year-end forecasts were made, further weakening net export prospects abroad. It is not clear, moreover, that many forecasts allowed for as large a constant-price swing in the U.S. deficit as we believe could occur.

These considerations raise a disturbing possibility. The rest of the OECD is much too close to the prospect of a real growth rate below 2 percent—a growth recession by any reasonable definition. The direct impact on the U.S. external deficit of slower foreign growth is illustrated in table 3-1. Model calculations suggest that 1 percent slower foreign growth could enlarge the deficit by as much as $20 billion to $30 billion over four years. Indirect effects must also be considered. Slower foreign growth could reduce interest rates abroad and thus tend to prop up the dollar. A growth recession starting in other OECD economies could have highly adverse effects on developing countries, many of which have fragile economies at present. Debt servicing is placing great strains on some of them, especially on their political stability. By eroding the ability of those countries to keep up their exports at the same time that the U.S. market would be less open to imports, a slowdown in Europe and Japan could exacerbate the debt crisis and threaten the liquidity of the world's private financial institutions. Even without financial instability, more sluggish growth outside the United States could damage confidence, causing investment to sag below its current mediocre rate. The world economy could slip into recession before natural corrective forces and belated policy adjustments buoyed it up. And if activity in the rest of the world fell off substantially, the improvement in the U.S. current balance projected earlier would be greatly reduced.

A growth recession abroad is not sure to happen. It is not even the single most probable outcome. Nonetheless, it is a distinct possibility and as of mid-1987 is a significant risk facing the world economy, threatening more dire results than the failure to achieve an orderly shrinkage of the U.S. external deficit.

For completeness, we should also note the argument that a sudden sharp decline in the dollar is a major threat to world economic recovery. Subscribers to this view contend that if exchange markets became persuaded that an additional large fall in the dollar is required for external balance, the currency could enter another period of steep declines. A more worrying possibility is that unease could spread to other financial (that is, stock and bond) markets. That would be more probable to the degree it appeared that the United States was failing to control and correct its structural budget deficit. Foreign holders of U.S. securities could decide that yields were insufficient to compensate them for the probability of further falls in the dollar. As the United States will need to borrow over $100 billion a year from foreigners for the foreseeable future, an incipient drying-up of the flow of foreign funds could push up interest rates, sharply if on a large scale.

The Federal Reserve would then be presented with a dilemma. On the one hand, if the Fed bowed to market pressures and tightened policy so that short-term rates followed the rise in long-term rates, continued real growth in the U.S. economy could be threatened. On the other hand, if the Fed tried to keep short-term rates down by, in effect, monetizing more of the federal deficit, it could inflame expectations of a vicious spiral of capital outflow, depreciation, and inflation.

We believe that the risks of a financial market crisis of this sort, precipitating a slowdown in the United States, are not inconsequential. Indeed, the continued fall in the dollar over the first quarter of 1987, combined with some "snugging" of interest rates by the Federal Reserve in April, contributed to a significant increase in U.S. long-term interest rates, which was likely to have a dampening effect on interest-sensitive sectors of the economy.

In any case, there is little need to debate which of the various unpleasant possibilities is the one to fear most. They all point to similar policy prescriptions: cooperative measures aimed at facilitating correction of imbalances while maintaining growth at home and abroad.

International Policy Cooperation

The world economic situation in 1987 illustrates starkly the dilemmas inherent in a world of politically independent nation-states whose economies have become increasingly interdependent. Individual nations have de jure sovereignty: decisions about policies can be made independently of what other governments want. Yet de facto each government has a limited ability to control its national economy. Its policy actions leak abroad to affect other countries. And foreign governments' policies spill over into the home economy.

Collective action is extraordinarily difficult. However, intergovernmental cooperation can be mutually beneficial—especially in situations of generalized imbalance in the world economy. A jointly agreed statement of goals and the policies to foster the goals could support each country's individual actions. And cooperation could create the climate of confidence, and of stability in expectations, needed to prevent either a recession or a resumption of rapid inflation.

The finance ministers of Canada, France, Japan, the United Kingdom, the United States, and West Germany met to discuss the international economic situation at the Louvre in Paris in February 1987. The leaders of those same countries, as well of Italy, met in Venice in June for their thirteenth summit meeting and reaffirmed their goal of macroeconomic policy cooperation. Although these meetings were welcome initiatives, substantially they fell well short of meaningful cooperation on the scale we believe is required. Promised German tax reductions are modest and will not be implemented until 1988. The original Japanese budget proposal for fiscal year 1987 was restrictive, not expansionary. But a supplementary spending package amounting to 6 trillion yen (about 1.8 percent of Japan's GNP) was announced just before the Venice summit. The spending package does not require Diet approval; however, the details on financing the package and the overall budget were still to be worked out with the Diet at the time of this writing.

The announcements made after the Louvre meeting that governments will "foster stability of exchange rates around current levels" could be, like the Baker-Miyazawa statement of October 1986, little more than an official hope that the exchange markets will avoid further downward pressure on the dollar for the time being. If the words turn out to be underpinned by commitments to prevent further dollar depreciation, the agreement is likely to prove fragile. Reduction of the large external imbalances among the major countries cannot be attained, we have argued, without eventual further dollar depreciation and substantial and sustained changes in relative growth rates. If participating governments try to stabilize exchange rates around the levels of mid-1987, moreover, they may be forced to adjust their monetary policies to meet that external goal rather than to meet their output and inflation objectives—a reversal of priorities that would not, and should not, command domestic political support. We outline below the elements of a viable and efficacious scheme of cooperation.

The beginning of wisdom in thinking about international cooperation in the current circumstances is to recognize that a correction of the U.S. external deficit—however it is achieved—will have deflationary effects on economic activity outside the United States. It is essential, therefore, that the governments of other industrial countries acknowledge their responsibility and capacity for maintaining the growth of domestic demand in the face of that deflationary impulse. They need to do so in more concrete ways than any seen hitherto. Ideally, foreign governments would seek to attain somewhat higher growth rates for their real GNPs than the below-potential rates that characterized 1982–86.

At present, individual foreign countries are reluctant to initiate expansionary action on their own, despite some vague commitments. They fear such actions, taken in isolation, would generate risks that outweigh any expected benefits.

To some extent governments are fighting the last war (and perhaps the next). In the late 1970s, the focus of macroeconomic policies was on the need to dampen inflationary expectations. Given the changed circumstances of the world economy, it is now no less important to recognize the importance of expectations about output growth. Like inflation, growth in real economic activity is dependent on expectations and endogenous to the current economic situation. Economies' supply capacities—in particular, the additions to capacity resulting from new investment—fluctuate with the state of expectations about, and confidence in, economic policies. If governments could credibly commit themselves to sustainable growth targets for output (subject to an inflation constraint), expectations about the economic environment would be substantially improved.

It is difficult for individual governments acting alone to have a major effect on expectations and confidence when the world economy is so interdependent. Collective commitments, and jointly agreed actions supporting those commitments, should be much more convincing and successful.

Differing views exist, of course, about the balance of risks. Foreign governments are very concerned about the U.S. budgetary situation and what it portends for future inflation and currency instability. The bloated federal budget deficit—the largest part of which is now structural, not cyclical—would almost certainly entail excess demand in the United States if it persisted while the external deficit was greatly reduced or eliminated. The U.S. government needs to acknowledge that point and accept that actions by foreign governments to maintain demand abroad depend on credible further cuts in the U.S. budget deficit. No less important, foreign governments should acknowledge that a rapid decline in the U.S. budget deficit in the absence of actions to maintain demand abroad could bring about world recession.

Given these considerations, the outlines of a mutually beneficial agreement among the major industrial countries can be readily identified. Such an agreement would have five main features. First, all participating governments would commit themselves to the goal of reducing the large current-account imbalances presently troubling the world economy.

That means, in particular, large reductions in the U.S. deficit and counterpart reductions by those OECD countries whose surpluses are inappropriately large in relation to the size of their economies.[6] Second, foreign governments would agree to take timely policy actions to maintain the growth of output as external imbalances are adjusted. Third, the United States would commit itself to a change in the mix of its policies to reduce future structural budget deficits. Fourth, the United States and other governments would announce their expectations—a "cooperative presumption"—about a lower exchange value of the dollar that they regard as consistent with the preceding goals and policies. This presumption would be stated in the form of a broad range, not a single number. Fifth, governments would once again renounce protectionism and renew their commitment to examine trade policy problems cooperatively.

The parts of such an agreement are closely interlinked. Few of the implied policies could stand alone because each would depend for its effectiveness on the other parts of the package. Similarly, while there is something in the package that each participating government would find difficult, there are also features each should want.

Some foreign governments, for example, have implied that the dollar is already undervalued and that they would find it hard to accept a further dollar depreciation. In February 1987, the United States appeared to accommodate this view with the statement at the Paris meeting of finance ministers that current exchange rates were appropriate. Yet the results summarized above strongly suggest that rectification of the U.S. external deficit in combination with sustainable growth targets will require some further depreciation. This requirement cannot be avoided by cutting the U.S. budget deficit. Indeed, a reduction in the budget deficit would by itself reduce credit demand and activity in the United States and thereby lower interest rates, which normally would lead to a dollar depreciation. (After all, the combination of the federal deficit and tight money largely caused the external deficit through its effects on the dollar's exchange value.) The desired tightening of fiscal policy in the United States would

6. While the U.S. current-account deficit in 1986 was 3.3 percent of GNP, several OECD countries had current-account surpluses as large or larger as a proportion of GNP. Four of them—Japan (4.2 percent), Germany (3.6), the Netherlands (4.3), and Switzerland (5.8)—have experienced surpluses for some years; their combined surplus in 1986 was roughly equal to the U.S. deficit. Outside the OECD, Taiwan is one country with what seems an egregiously large current-account surplus (16.3 percent of GNP in 1985 and 24.5 percent in 1986).

therefore tend to strengthen foreign currencies, unless accompanied by a U.S. monetary contraction. Combined fiscal and monetary contraction in the United States would, however, precipitate a U.S. recession, which, given the policies currently pursued by foreign governments, foreign economies could not withstand.

A cooperative presumption about a moderate further decline in the dollar (with understandings about the currencies against which it was most likely to occur) is therefore an important part of any viable agreement. The participating governments need not make—and could not credibly do so—an absolute commitment to maintain dollar exchange rates within the ranges given by their agreement. Rather, the announced ranges would be their own rough estimate of where the economic fundamentals should be moving the exchange value of the dollar over 1987–90, taking into account the implications of their own joint policy actions. In the judgment of the participating governments, the announced ranges would be consistent with more balanced external positions. Financial markets would then have better information about the joint expectations of governments and would also be aware that departures of the dollar's exchange value from this range would trigger discussions among governments of whether exchange market intervention or the adjustment of the relative stance of monetary policies was required.

The path of the dollar's exchange value depends critically on the other parts of the agreement. For example, if governments could agree on how much current-account imbalances should be reduced, then the rates of demand growth to which the European and Japanese governments could commit would vary inversely with the additional appreciation of the currencies of surplus countries. If the United States restrained domestic demand growth by fiscal restriction on or near the Gramm-Rudman-Hollings path while the surplus economies targeted nominal GNP growth of not less than 5 or 6 percent, the presumptive additional dollar depreciation might be set in a range of 10 to 25 percent. If this expectation were regarded as credible, financial markets might then rapidly mark down the dollar by 10 to 15 percent, with the rest of the expected depreciation over 1987–90 being compensated for by nominal interest rate differentials.

A contingent presumption of this sort about further dollar depreciation does not imply "target zones" for exchange rates. Moreover, in the absence of an agreement about rates of demand growth and the other parts of the package, it would *not* be desirable to announce such a presumption (much less imply that actions would be taken to keep exchange rates in conformity with such a presumption). The stated commitment of governments to maintain current exchange rates, made in February 1987 and repeated several times later in the spring, was not credibly supported by the vague or small initiatives announced in actual policies. Much more vigorous fiscal policy action would be needed to validate anything like the exchange rates of spring 1987.

Foreign governments could take several combinations of policy actions that would support agreed output and current-account targets. Some fiscal expansion through tax cuts would be helpful in promoting the desired adjustment in payments imbalances. Fiscal expansion would raise demand and imports in foreign economies without necessarily leading to depreciation of their currencies, as monetary expansion would. Many foreign governments are reluctant to undertake fiscal expansion, however, because of concern about the medium-term outlook for their public sector budget deficits.

A synchronized easing of fiscal policy abroad, if it increased real output, would not have much adverse effect on actual budget positions. Yet national governments, accustomed to weighing the effect of policy changes made in isolation, are reluctant to accept that point. Many Europeans, moreover, remain pessimistic about the ability of their economies to respond to a demand stimulus with real output. The pessimism is illogical: governments do not lose sleep over the inflationary implications of export demand, so if export demand weakens, there is no reason why they should worry about the inflationary implications of domestic demand. Nonetheless, governments' concerns about their debt positions suggest that at least part of the foreign expansion will have to come about through monetary policy.

The relative stance of monetary policies in the United States and abroad is important. The greater foreign monetary expansion is in relation to foreign fiscal expansion, the easier U.S. monetary policy must be in order not to impede the necessary additional depreciation of the dollar. Governments would have to adjust their monetary policies in relation to one another, depending on what exchange markets were doing and how fast the swing was occurring in current-account imbalances. Declared targets for monetary policy should be conditional, with their dependency on outcomes made clear to guide public expectations.

An environment in which foreign growth was being maintained and the U.S. external deficit was coming down would be the best one possible in which to undertake the necessary correction of the U.S. structural budget deficit. Indeed, as was confirmed by deliberations at the Venice summit, a credible U.S. plan of action to reduce the budget deficit is almost certainly a sine qua non for any international agreement. The governments of Germany and Japan, in particular, would not take part in any jointly agreed actions whose global consequences they considered inflationary. Bolstering demand in the rest of the world when domestic demand is strong in the United States could risk inflation not too many years ahead. A shift in the balance of domestic demands between the United States and other countries is much more likely to command acceptance than a simple boost to total world demand.

Unfortunately, the government of the United States has no credibility whatever on this subject. Administration officials have responded to overseas criticism of the budget deficit since at least 1982 by agreeing with it and blaming Congress. Foreign governments have not failed to notice that general lip service is paid in the United States—by the White House even more than the Congress—to reducing the budget deficit, while the political deadlock that perpetuates it drags on. In effect, all parts of the U.S. government care about the budget deficit a little bit but not enough to exercise courageous political leadership.

Fiscal correction in the United States will be impossible to attain without a domestic political compromise. And some form of tax increase will be essential. Not only is that true, but foreign governments know it is true. The 1986 tax reform legislation and the president's preoccupation with the negative incentive effects of high income tax rates suggest that additional revenues will probably have to come from indirect taxes. The traditional approach of raising taxes on items with low price elasticities of demand—for example, tobacco and alcoholic beverages—has much to recommend it. Concern with energy conservation and long-run oil consumption might argue, for example, for an additional tax on gasoline (to be channeled into general revenues, not spent on more highways).

The key point is that foreign governments would find Treasury Secretary James Baker more persuasive if he had a carrot to offer as well as a stick. A credible plan for a tax hike in his back pocket would be a more winning negotiating chip than thinly veiled threats to let the dollar depreciate. Furthermore, the tax rise would be easier to sell to domestic political constituencies in the United States if it were part of an international agreement in which other governments were committed to doing their share.

We are not sanguine that genuine actions promoting international economic cooperation will soon be adopted. An international agreement along these lines is economic common sense, but it is a political house of cards. No part stands up on its own; the package can be drawn up and implemented only if each major country agrees to make its contribution. If an important player holds out or withdraws one of his cards, the whole edifice will come fluttering down.

The imagination and will required for international agreements, and the sheer hard work of crafting the details, tend to be mustered only in times of crisis. Although the dangers currently facing the world economy are real, statesmen and bureaucrats are probably not yet frightened enough to do the constructive thing. If the situation begins to deteriorate, we must all hope that their capacity for fright and foresight measures up to the imperious needs of the times.

CHAPTER FOUR

Sustainability and the Decline of the Dollar

PAUL R. KRUGMAN

WHEN THE DOLLAR peaked in the first quarter of 1985, almost nobody believed that it could maintain that level indefinitely. If the dollar stayed that strong, the U.S. current account, already massively in deficit, would deteriorate further. The situation could not continue forever. The only real question was how to view a strength that all agreed was temporary. Did that strength represent a rational market response to the underlying fundamentals, or was it a case of financial markets gone awry? Would the dollar fall gradually, at a rate comparable to the interest rate differential between the United States and other nations, or would it fall rapidly and suffer a "hard landing"?

When the dollar was at its peak, I proposed, as a way to approach these issues, a simple calculation to assess whether the strength of the dollar "made sense"—whether it could be viewed as the result of rational investor decisions, given the differences in interest rates that many thought explained its strength.[1] The calculation appeared to show that the strong dollar did not, in fact, make sense and that investors had failed to appreciate how fast the dollar would have to decline if the United States were not to run up impossible levels of foreign debt. The implications were that the dollar was stronger than fundamentals could warrant and that financial markets would be forced to revise their expectations, precipitating a sharp decline in the dollar.

This paper was originally presented under the title "Has the Dollar Fallen Enough?" at the Brookings Conference on the U.S. Current Account, January 1987. The change of title reflects the way the original analysis was overtaken by events. I would like to thank Peter Hooper of the Federal Reserve Board of Governors for invaluable help with the numbers, and Michael Dooley of the International Monetary Fund for helpful discussion; responsibility for errors remains mine.
1. Paul R. Krugman, "Is the Strong Dollar Sustainable?" Working Paper 1644 (Cambridge, Mass.: National Bureau of Economic Research, June 1985).

As it turned out, the dollar did decline sharply. However, by late 1986 the decline had not yet produced a large improvement in the U.S. current account, and at the exchange rates that prevailed at the time, few analysts believed that the U.S. current account would move anywhere close to balance. Thus in late 1986, the question of early 1985 was still with us, although in modified form: did the fact that the dollar's decline had stopped short of the level that would balance the U.S. current account "make sense"? Simply put, had the dollar fallen enough?

The initial draft of this paper was written at the beginning of 1987 and has been somewhat overtaken by events. It concluded, using the same test developed in 1985, that the exchange rate of late 1986 was *not* sustainable, that the dollar had not fallen enough. Although the dollar had fallen dramatically, at late 1986 levels the United States would have continued to accumulate large quantities of foreign debt. Thus the dollar was bound to fall. Yet the real interest differential, which had been invoked in 1985 to explain the strong dollar, had virtually disappeared. Since the dollar would necessarily fall over time, and investors in the United States were not being compensated for this necessary decline by higher returns, they should not have been willing to continue financing the U.S. current-account deficit. When investors realized their predicament, the dollar once again plunged, confirming the conclusion of my paper but also rendering it less than startling. Thus the paper has now become more of a retrospective than a forecast. The focus is now on the method of analysis and on the implications of the conclusion that the exchange markets have repeatedly made mistakes that could be diagnosed using simple tests on readily available data.

The paper is in three parts. The first part reviews the issue of the sustainability of an exchange rate and compares the situation in early 1985 with that of late 1986. The second part develops an algebraic analysis for testing whether the exchange rate makes sense, and applies the analysis both to the historical peak of the dollar and to the situation in the spring of 1987. A brief back-of-the-envelope calculation asks whether the dollar needs to fall still further. Finally, the third part discusses a few possible qualifications to the analysis.

The Sustainability Issue

When the dollar was at its peak, the question of sustainability was, loosely speaking, how long can this go on? The question turned out to be more subtle than was generally realized. In late 1986, the question was whether the dollar had fallen far enough; loosely speaking, had it reached a level that could persist for some time? Conceptually, the two questions are identical. The fundamental issues, and the subtleties, are the same; the difference is the particular facts of the situation.

Alternative Concepts of Sustainability

In early 1985 it was clear that the level of the dollar implied continuing massive current-account deficits. Even now, according to the results of the January 1987 Brookings workshop, the current level of the dollar means sizable deficits for the foreseeable future. However, in a world of mobile capital a country need not run a balanced current account at any given point. The question of sustainability is whether the deficits are in some sense feasible. Ultimately, it is a question of the ability of the United States to finance its deficits. The subtlety comes in the choice of a time horizon.

Most discussion approaches the issue of the sustainability of exchange rates in one of two ways. While both are superficially plausible, both miss the point.

The first approach asks what would happen if the dollar were to remain at the current real exchange rate forever. That approach quickly makes it clear that the current exchange rate is not feasible. The current level of the dollar implies a persistent U.S. deficit on goods and services other than factor income. As long as the real interest rate that the United States pays on external debt exceeds the rate of growth of the U.S. economy, the implication is that U.S. debt grows ever larger relative to the nation's ability to repay. Sooner or later the borrowing must stop. The dollar is not sustainable, if sustainability means that it can remain at its current level without ever declining.

This approach misses the point, however, because the criterion of being able to hold the exchange rate forever at its current level is too strong. Suppose, as many argued when the dollar was strong, that a gradual decline in the currency could limit the growth in debt to feasible levels.[2] Then although the dollar must eventually fall, the current level or something close to it might persist for a long time. Most people would

2. See Peter Isard and Lois Stekler, "U.S. International Capital Flows and the Dollar," *Brookings Papers on Economic Activity, 1:1985*, pp. 219–36.

view an assertion that the dollar need decline by only a few percent a year over the near future as an assertion that the current level is basically sustainable.

The alternative approach is to ask whether the current-account deficits could be financed for a certain limited period. Exercises that project U.S. deficits over the next five years invariably suggest that the current rate is sustainable because the U.S. economy starts with little net external debt and can clearly accumulate much more before the size of that debt becomes infeasible.

The problem with this approach is that history does not end after five years. Suppose that at the current exchange rate the United States could finance the resulting current-account deficit for eight years, but that after that the dollar would have to fall steeply because of financing constraints. It is unlikely then that the dollar could actually remain strong for the first eight years. The knowledge of an impending fall in year nine would drive the dollar down in year eight; if investors anticipated that fall, they would try to get out of the dollar in year seven, and so on. If investors fully anticipated the whole sequence of events, the prospect of future financing constraints, even many years distant, should affect the value of the dollar now.

The dollar need not fall immediately to a level that prevents any accumulation of foreign debt. As long as investors earn a rate of return on dollar assets that exceeds the rate on assets in other currencies by as much as the expected decline, they will not try to get out of dollar-denominated assets, even if they expect the dollar to decline. Even with fully informed investors, the dollar can therefore stay above its long-run sustainable level when the U.S. interest rate exceeds foreign rates. It is possible to envisage an equilibrium path along which the current account is at first in large deficit, but then, with the dollar declining gradually, at the same rate as the interest differential, the deficit falls fast enough to prevent infeasible debt accumulation. In this case, which is typical in theoretical models of exchange rates, the current level of the dollar should be regarded as sustainable in the relevant sense.

Suppose, however, that if the dollar were to decline at the interest differential, debt accumulation could not be kept within the limits of feasibility. Then the dollar must in fact fall faster. If investors realized that the capital losses on their dollar holdings would exceed the extra interest they were receiving, they would try to get out of dollars, driving the dollar lower. If investors keep their dollar holdings, it is because the market fails to anticipate how fast the currency must decline. The concept of sustainability that underlies both my 1985 paper and the current paper is that an exchange rate is unsustainable if the currency must decline *faster than the market now expects,* so that, sooner or later, the market will be forced to revise its expectations, leading to a sudden fall in the dollar. A currency is unsustainable, in other words, when the expectations that sustain its current level cannot be fulfilled and must be revised.

Suppose, for example, that I am able to conclude in the spring of 1987, by looking at economic fundamentals, that the dollar must decline 15 percent in real terms over the next five years. At the same time, there is hardly any real interest differential between the United States and other industrial countries. Dollar assets are thus a poor investment, although the market apparently does not realize it. When investors do realize the extent of capital losses that they face on their dollar assets, they will try to shift out of dollars, leading to a sudden decline in the exchange rate.

How do I determine that the dollar must fall faster than the market expects? A model, developed below, is required. But first I need to assess the nature of the constraints on current-account financing.

Constraints on Long-Run Current-Account Deficits

A path for the current account will be infeasible if it leads to the accumulation of too much external debt. The question is, what is too much?

Infinity, obviously, is too much. If the current level of the dollar depends on an expectation that the exchange rate will decline so slowly that U.S. debt will forever grow faster than the nation's ability to repay, that expectation must be wrong. Such was the case both in early 1985 and in late 1986 (see below). The expectations sustaining the dollar would have implied runaway growth in U.S. foreign debt.

Even when debt accumulation is not runaway, there may still be some limit on how large a claim on the U.S. economy foreigners will be willing to hold. The limit could stem from either of two situations. First, holdings of U.S. debt could become too large a share of foreigners' portfolios. Second, foreigners could come to regard the United States as too heavily indebted relative to its ability to repay.

Peter Isard and Lois Stekler have emphasized the portfolio side. In a paper written when the dollar was peaking, they concluded that a gradual decline would allow foreign claims on the United States to stabilize at about 10 percent of foreigners' net worth, which does not seem a forbidding number (although it was probably understated).[3]

Emphasizing the portfolio constraint suggests that small countries should be virtually unconstrained in their ability to borrow, since even Brazilian and Mexican debt amount to fractions of 1 percent of world wealth. Since creditors do seem to care how large their claims on these countries are, it seems that indebtedness relative to ability to pay—as measured, say, by gross national product—is the right criterion.

The point is that when a country's debt becomes large enough relative to its GNP, the burden of debt service becomes significant, and there is a real incentive to default. Because investors are aware of those incentives, the supply of foreign financing drops off when external debt gets too large relative to the size of the economy. Such a prospect seems inconceivable for the United States, but it might look less so if U.S. net foreign debt were currently $2 trillion. The United States is not Mexico, but if the dollar had remained at its early 1985 level, U.S. indebtedness relative to GNP might have been as large as Mexico's within less than a decade.

Based on this line of argument, I conclude that the most relevant measure of the size of U.S. foreign debt is its ratio to GNP, and that the experience of problem debtors may be used as a guide to what constitutes an infeasible level.

Early 1985 and Late 1986

Before I turn to an explicit model for assessing sustainability, it may be helpful to review some basic facts about the dollar. In particular, it is useful to contrast the real exchange rate and the real interest rate at the dollar's peak and after the fall. Because of issues of data availability, the periods that I compare are the first quarter of 1985 and the third quarter of 1986. The dramatic further fall of the dollar in early 1987 seems to confirm the diagnosis presented here, but requires that we make a rough attempt to update the conclusions.

The basic structure of the quantitative exercises in this paper derives from the Federal Reserve's Multicountry Model (MCM), which is based on only five countries: the United States, Canada, Germany, Japan, and the United Kingdom.[4] The problems raised by this limitation are dis-

3. Ibid.
4. See Hali J. Edison, Jaime R. Marquez, and Ralph W. Tryon, "The Structure and Properties of the FRB Multicountry Model," *Economic Modelling*, vol. 4 (April 1987).

Table 4-1. *Real Exchange Rates, U.S. Dollar, 1985:1 and 1986:3*[a]

Currency	1985:1	1986:3
Canadian dollar	.057	.058
Deutsche mark	.648	.227
Yen	.253	−.242
Pound sterling	.668	.281
Four-currency average	.458	.096

Source: International Monetary Fund, *International Financial Statistics*.
a. Logarithmic changes from 1980 average, deflated by consumer price changes. The four-country average uses weights derived from the Multicountry Model of the Federal Reserve Board staff.

cussed in the final section of the paper. For now, I ignore them and treat this five-country group as if it represented the world.

Table 4-1 shows real exchange rates, using consumer price indexes (CPIs) as deflators, of the dollar against the currencies of Canada, Germany, Japan, and the United Kingdom in 1985:1 and 1986:3. The rates are expressed as logarithmic differences from the 1980 average. Also shown is an average rate, using the MCM weights.

The table shows that for all these countries except Canada, the slide of the dollar since early 1985 has reversed almost 80 percent of the rise from 1980 to the dollar's peak. Because the dollar in 1980 was weak relative to its average in the 1970s, the average dollar exchange rate in 1986:3 was more or less at a level that would have been regarded as an equilibrium in the early 1980s. Even before the recent slide one could no longer speak unambiguously of a strong dollar.

Recently there has been considerable questioning of the use of exchange rate measures that include only industrial countries and that fail to take account of structural change within economies. These critiques may be important, but a discussion will be postponed until the last section of the paper.

Another issue is that of competition from developing countries, particularly the newly industrialized countries (NICs), whose currencies have not appreciated against the dollar. Leaving aside highly publicized numbers that fail to correct for inflation differences, I agree with other analysts that adding the NICs does lead to the conclusion that the dollar is still somewhat above its range for the 1970s.[5] However, the NICs by and large do not have free movement of private capital; thus the

5. See chapter 2 and Martin Feldstein and Philippe Bacchetta, "How Far Has the Dollar Fallen?" Working Paper 2122 (Cambridge, Mass.: National Bureau of Economic Research, January 1987).

Table 4-2. *Real Interest Rates, United States, Canada, Germany, Japan, United Kingdom, 1985:1 and 1986:3*

Country	1985:1	1986:3
Canada	8.6	5.6
Germany	5.2	5.8
Japan	4.5	4.0
United Kingdom	4.8	6.9
Four-country average	5.5	5.6
United States	8.3	5.9
Differential between U.S. rate and four-country average	2.8	0.3

Sources: Interest rates are long-term government bond rates at constant maturity, supplied by Federal Reserve Board staff. Inflation rates are CPI change over previous year. The four-country average uses weights from the MCM.

comparison between expected and feasible rates of exchange rate change is not relevant, and NIC currencies should not be included in the exchange rate index for calculating sustainability.

Table 4-2 shows estimated real interest rates for the MCM countries in 1985:1 and 1986:3; the real rate is the difference between long-term government bond rates and the rate of consumer price inflation over the previous year. While alternative measures might be constructed, the basic picture accords with common wisdom. In early 1985 U.S. real interest rates were considerably higher than those in other industrial countries. By late 1986, the differential had virtually vanished against all countries except Japan, and the average U.S. premium was only a fraction of a percent.

The contrast between 1985:1 and 1986:3 can be summarized quickly. In 1985:1 the U.S. dollar was very strong by historical standards, and its strength was supported by a high real interest rate relative to rates in other countries. In 1986:3 the dollar was back to historical levels, and the real interest differential was also absent.

Unfortunately, the decline in the dollar to historical levels was not expected to return the U.S. balance of payments to historical normalcy. Virtually all estimates, including those of the January 1987 Brookings workshop, were that maintaining the exchange rate at late 1986 levels would produce only a small decline in the current-account deficit at first, and that the deficit would then again begin to widen. I discuss the reasons for this conclusion, and its plausibility, in the last part of the paper. Given this expectation, however, the question was whether even the depreciated dollar was sustainable.

Calculating Sustainability

To repeat, an exchange rate is unsustainable if it must decline faster than the market expects. Ideally, one would calculate the exchange rate path from the best available model and contrast it with market expectations. Unfortunately, no exchange rate models are reliable, especially because irrational speculative bubbles can drive the exchange rate far from its equilibrium path. A more modest testing procedure is to ask how fast the market appears to expect the exchange rate to decline, then to calculate the consequences of this rate of decline for U.S. debt accumulation and ask whether the result appears feasible. If it does not, then I conclude that the exchange rate is not sustainable.

The procedure described does *not* involve an explicit model of the exchange rate. It does not provide a way of forecasting the actual path of the dollar. All that it does is provide a warning device, indicating that the current exchange rate is sustained by expectations that are bound to be disappointed. How and when the reckoning comes are beyond the procedure's scope.

Current Accounts and Debt Accumulation

The algebra of my test focuses on the behavior of the ratio of debt to GNP over time. Let D_t be the ratio of U.S. external debt to GNP at the end of year t. Then this ratio will evolve over time according to the following rule:

$$(1) \qquad D_t = (1 + r - g)D_{t-1} + B_t,$$

where r is the real interest rate, g is the rate of GNP growth, and B is the ratio of the noninterest current-account deficit to GNP. Note that for the evolution of the debt-GNP ratio, what matters is not the current account as usually measured, but a current account adjusted for both inflation and growth.

If lags are neglected, the noninterest current account depends on the real exchange rate and other factors:

$$(2) \qquad B_t = K + bE_t,$$

where E_t is the natural logarithm of the exchange rate and K is a term that encompasses all other effects. The view that the U.S. current-account deficit will remain negative despite the return of the dollar to historical levels means that K has shifted since 1980; however, my working assumption is that K will be constant from now on.

To assess sustainability, the question is whether market expectations are feasible. I construct a *hypothetical* path for the exchange rate, in which it declines only at the rate that the market appears to expect, as proxied by the real interest differential. This hypothetical path is not necessarily the one that the exchange rate will actually follow; indeed, if I conclude that the exchange rate is not sustainable, I am asserting precisely that it cannot follow this path. Thus, to reemphasize the point, this is an "as if" exercise, not an attempt to model the exchange rate.

If the exchange rate declines by the interest differential,

$$(3) \qquad\qquad E_{t+1} = E_t - (r - r^*),$$

where r^* is the foreign real interest rate.

Equations 1 through 3 define a small dynamic system that can be simulated forward to track the path of debt accumulation implied by the market expectations that sustain the current exchange rate. When the initial exchange rate implies growing debt, but the exchange rate is expected to decline, this framework essentially lets one watch the race between declining trade deficits and growing debt service.

There are two questions to ask about this race. First, who will win it? Will the trade deficit decline quickly enough to prevent debt from growing without limit? If not, the exchange rate can immediately be declared unsustainable. Given the structure of the model, the condition for explosive debt growth is a simple one. From equations 1 and 2 we have

$$(4) \qquad\qquad D_t = (1 + r - g)D_{t-1} + K + bE_t.$$

Taking first differences of equation 4 gives

$$(5) \qquad D_{t+1} - D_t = (1 + r - g)(D_t - D_{t-1}) + b(\dot{E}_{t+1} - E_t)$$
$$= (1 + r - g)(D_t - D_{t-1}) - b(r - r^*).$$

Rearranging equation 5 gives

$$(6) \quad (D_{t+1} - D_t) - (D_t - D_{t-1}) = (r - g)(D_t - D_{t-1}) - b(r - r^*).$$

If the right-hand side of equation 6 is initially positive, the rise in the debt-GNP ratio will actually accelerate over time; if the right-hand side is negative, the rise will slow and eventually reverse. Thus the criterion for runaway debt growth is

$$(7) \qquad\qquad D_t - D_{t-1} > b(r - r^*)/(r - g)$$

at the initial period.

Suppose that debt growth is not runaway. Then the question is whether the maximum debt-GNP ratio implied by market expectations is feasible. Here there is no rigid criterion. Presumably, however, it is difficult to contemplate the prospect of U.S. external indebtedness as large relative to GNP as that of Latin American nations. The timing and size of the peak of the debt-GNP ratio can be calculated analytically, but it will suffice to present numerical calculations.

Parameter Values and Initial Conditions

The model has only three parameters: K, the intercept in the trade balance equation; b, the change in the current account as a percentage of GNP that results from a 1 percent exchange rate change; and g, the long-run growth rate of the economy.

The MCM implies a sensitivity of the current account to the exchange rate of approximately 0.1—that is, a 10 percent depreciation improves the current account by 1 percent of GNP. Also, simulations with that model indicate that holding exchange rates at their 1986:3 level would eventually reduce the noninterest current-account deficit to roughly 2 percent of GNP. Letting E be the logarithmic change since 1980 (presented in table 4-1) implies the balance of payments equation

$$(8) \qquad\qquad B_t = .0104 + 0.1E_t.$$

Given the exchange rate numbers in table 4-1, this equation implies that if the dollar had remained at its 1985:1 level, the noninterest current account would eventually have moved into a deficit of more than 5.5 percent of GNP. It also implies that, from its level in 1986:3, the dollar would need to depreciate a further 20 percent or more to stabilize U.S. external debt.

For the long-run rate of growth of the economy, I assume 3 percent. This estimate is probably on the high side, so that the results reported below are if anything too optimistic about sustainability.

The model requires four initial conditions: the U.S. real interest rate r, the foreign real interest rate r^*, the exchange rate E, and the initial debt stock D. These initial conditions were examined at two points, 1985:1 and 1986:3. Values of the first three were taken from the data in tables 4-1 and 4-2. The debt stock issue is less straightforward, both because of unreliable data and because of the issue of timing. The balance of payments equation captures long-run adjustment, but in reality, as

Table 4-3. *Parameters and Initial Conditions*

Variable	1985:1	1986:3
K	.0104	.0104
b	.1	.1
g	.03	.03
r	.083	.059
r*	.055	.056
E	.458	.096
D	0	.1

Americans are once again finding out, trade adjustment is slow. Thus by the time the post-1985 dollar decline has any effect on the trade balance, the United States will have run up a lot more foreign debt. Rather than tackle these timing issues carefully, I will somewhat arbitrarily set D for 1985:1 at 0 and for 1986:3 at 0.1, reflecting the likely debt accumulation before the noninterest current account has fully responded to the weaker dollar.

The parameters and initial conditions are summarized in table 4-3, showing the values for both 1985:1 and 1986:3.

Numerical Results

The first test of sustainability is whether the accumulation of debt will be runaway. For both 1985:1 and 1986:3 the dollar fails this test. That is, given the numbers I have used here, if the dollar had declined no faster than the interest differential from its 1985 peak, the ratio of U.S. debt to GNP would have risen at an accelerating rate; the same is true starting from the third quarter of 1986. For 1985:1, we have

$$(9) \qquad D_t - D_{t-1} = K + bE_t = 0.0104 + 0.1 \times 0.4574 = 0.0581,$$

$$b(r - r^*)/(r - g) = 0.1 \times (0.083 - 0.055)/(0.083 - 0.030) = 0.053.$$

For 1986:3, the criterion is

$$(10) \qquad D_t - D_{t-1} = K + bE_t + (r - g)D_{t-1} = 0.0104 + 0.1 \times 0.096$$
$$+ (0.059 - 0.030) \times 0.1 = 0.0229,$$

$$b(r - r^*)/(r - g) = 0.1 \times (0.059 - 0.056)/(0.059 - 0.030) = 0.0103.$$

Given that the debt is runaway, there is no maximum debt-GNP ratio. It is still interesting, however, to track the rise in debt that would occur if the dollar fell no faster than the interest differential. Simulation of the system of equations 1–3 shows that if the exchange rate had fulfilled the market expectations of 1985:1, U.S. external debt would have risen to 61.6 percent of GNP after ten years. If the dollar were to fulfill the market expectations of 1986:3, external debt would rise to 38.8 percent of GNP after ten years.

Why did the dramatic fall in the dollar fail to correct the problem of unsustainability diagnosed in 1985? The answer is clear: in 1985 the dollar was too far above a permanently sustainable level to be justified by interest differentials; by late 1986 it was much closer to that ultimately sustainable level, but in the virtual absence of an interest differential, an exchange rate that produces any current-account deficit is not sustainable.

The dollar, of course, fell substantially between the third quarter of 1986 and the second quarter of 1987. I will not attempt to update the calculation based on the latest data, but simply note that a 10 percent fall in the exchange rate from the 1986:3 level, according to my equations, would produce an initial $D_t - D_{t-1}$ of 0.0129, which is still marginally in the runaway range. A 20 percent fall, however, would place the exchange rate comfortably inside the feasible range, and indeed imply only minimal debt accumulation once the lags have had time to work through. Given the uncertainty of the trade balance equation, one would not want to lean too heavily on these results; but they suggest that while there may still be some need for a further decline in the dollar (from the level in the spring of 1987), the clear-cut case against sustainability is no longer there.

Questions and Qualifications

The initial draft of this paper repeated the brashness of my 1985 paper by suggesting that, once again, the markets had it wrong; they had failed to understand the need for further dollar decline. Such a strong conclusion based on such a simple data analysis demands that at least a few questions be asked—even when, as in this case, the conclusion proves to be correct. The two questions that seem most relevant concern the pessimism about whether the current account can return to balance and the identification of the real interest differential with the expected rate of dollar decline.

The Current-Account Implications of Current Exchange Rates

Those who look at purchasing power parity, especially between industrial countries, tend to conclude that the dollar has if anything fallen too much. As table 4-1 shows, by late 1986 the real dollar was pretty much back to its pre-Reagan level. My conclusion that the 1986:3 dollar needed to fall further depends on my assertion that the 1985–86 decline would not be enough to restore current-account balance. The question is why that decline is insufficient.

Essentially, the forecast of a persistent current-account deficit by major trade models arises from an extrapolation of four factors that were important earlier in the 1980s. First is the faster growth of domestic demand in the United States than in other industrial countries from 1982 to 1985. According to the models that participated in the Brookings workshop, the relatively faster growth of U.S. demand in those years was a significant factor contributing to the growing deficit.[6] Second is the debt crisis, which led to reduced imports by LDCs, especially in Latin America. Third is the competition from newly industrializing countries—for example, Taiwan and South Korea—whose currencies have not risen against the dollar. Fourth is a secular depreciation in the exchange rate associated with any given trade balance, something that appears in all models either in the guise of a difference between export and import income elasticities or in some kind of trend term. These factors together apparently worsened the current account associated with any given level of the dollar's exchange value against industrial-country currencies by about 2 percent of U.S. GNP.

My conclusions about sustainability could be called into question if there were a prospect for a dramatic reversal of these factors in the future. If Europe were to experience a surging recovery, banks to regain confidence in Latin America, and the Korean won and the Taiwan dollar to experience massive appreciations, the need for further dollar decline would be substantially reduced.

Recall the point made earlier, however, that it would not make sense to include developing-country currencies in the exchange rate index

6. For further details, see chapters 2 and 3.

used for sustainability calculations because of the presence of capital and exchange controls. The sustainability test depends on a comparison of the rates of return on assets in different currencies with the necessary rate of currency decline. If there are capital controls, so that investors are not free to shift between the assets, the comparison makes no sense.

On the other side, some have argued that the U.S. competitive position is worse than the exchange rate indicates, because of productivity growth in U.S. competitors, especially Japan. Richard Marston notes that during the decade from 1973 to 1983, Japan's productivity growth in tradable sectors, and especially manufacturing, was much faster than it was in nontraded sectors.[7] As a result, real exchange rate indexes based on broad deflators, such as GNP or the CPI, understated the rise in Japanese competitiveness over that period. The productivity growth argument also seems to resolve the puzzle of Japan's current-account surplus. As table 4-1 shows, the yen never fell as much against the dollar as European currencies did, and has now risen well above historical levels. Yet Japan has run current-account surpluses as large relative to GNP as the deficits of the United States.

But although the productivity argument was valid for the 1970s, it does not seem to be borne out for the 1980s. From 1980 to the second quarter of 1986, Japan's wholesale price of manufactured goods fell 19 percent relative to its CPI. However, the U.S. wholesale manufactures price fell 15 percent relative to the CPI. While Japanese productivity growth in manufactures has continued to exceed that of the United States, the measured differential has narrowed, and the spectacularly poor U.S. productivity performance in other sectors has ensured that the productivity differential has no longer caused much bias in real exchange rate measures.[8]

It remains possible that in some way this measure does not entirely capture how much Japanese competitiveness has improved. Marston emphasizes differential productivity growth within the manufacturing sector, with Japan's advantage greatest in internationally competitive subsectors. Anecdotal evidence suggests Japanese gains in relative technological prowess and quality that may not be captured by the real

---

7. See Richard C. Marston, "Real Exchange Rates and Productivity Growth in the United States and Japan," Working Paper 1922 (Cambridge, Mass.: National Bureau of Economic Research, May 1986), p. 15.

8. See table 2-18 in chapter 2 for data on comparative manufacturing unit labor costs.

exchange rate numbers. It is certainly hard to believe that Japanese competitiveness vis-à-vis the United States is actually 20 percent worse than it was in 1980. However, this intuition cannot at present be quantified.

A final argument that, if true, would strengthen the case against sustainability is the view that the unprecedented size and persistence of the dollar's overvaluation did permanent harm to the U.S. competitive position. Richard Baldwin and I advanced a theoretical analysis along these lines in 1986, but so far there is no evidence that any such exotic model is needed.[9] Existing models are able to explain the persistence of the current-account deficit simply by a combination of the factors I have described plus long lags.[10]

Rejecting Open Interest Parity

A key assumption of my analysis here has been that of open interest parity, that is, that the interest differential is equal to the expected rate of change of the exchange rate. One reaction to the results would be to reject this assumption and argue that the expected rate of dollar depreciation is larger than the interest differential. This view receives some support from surveys of expectations, which have consistently indicated that investors expect a dollar decline steeper than the interest differential.[11]

But if investors expect the decline of the dollar to exceed the interest differential, they must expect capital losses on dollar assets to exceed any interest advantage. Why, then, are they willing to hold U.S. securities and indeed increase their holdings at a rate sufficient to finance the U.S. current-account deficit?

One explanation could be the safe-haven interpretation of capital flows to the United States. If political risk leads investors to fear expropriation of assets outside the United States, they might be willing to increase their claims on the United States despite expected capital losses. I have reviewed the problems with this explanation at length:

9. See Richard E. Baldwin and Paul R. Krugman, "Persistent Trade Effects of Large Exchange Rate Shocks," Working Paper 2017 (Cambridge, Mass.: National Bureau of Economic Research, August 1986).

10. See, for example, chapter 2.

11. See Jeffrey A. Frankel and Kenneth Froot, "Using Survey Data to Test Some Standard Propositions Regarding Exchange Rate Expectations," Working Paper 1672 (Cambridge, Mass.: National Bureau of Economic Research, July 1985).

essentially they boil down to the implausibility of such safe-haven considerations between the United States and other industrial countries.[12] It may be true that the United States is a favored destination for flight capital from third world nations; but if the dollar were actually expected to decline faster than the interest differential, industrial-country residents (including U.S. residents) would be moving their capital the other way. No such shift seems to be happening. Even if it were, it would mean that flight capital is financing more than all of the U.S. current-account deficit. It just does not seem possible that the United States has been receiving inflows of flight capital on a sustained basis of more than $100 billion a year.

Still unsolved is the puzzle of the difference between the survey results and actual asset returns. Finance theorists would simply note that what people say and what they actually believe and act upon are two different things. A more heterodox view would be that investors are subject to illusions about their own ability to outsmart the market. Perhaps each investor believes that he will be able to get out just before the dollar falls. It would not be the first time investors have made that mistake.

Conclusions

The approach used to assess sustainability in this paper, the model that implements that approach, and the data underlying that model are all far from satisfactory. The results should be trusted only when their qualitative character is extremely clear. Such was, in my view, the case when the dollar was at its peak. I also believe the case was still clear in late 1986.

In early 1985 the dollar was extremely strong, and the interest differential that was alleged by many economists to explain that strength was modest. The need for the dollar to decline fairly rapidly to avoid infeasible debt accumulation was or should have been apparent, and the interest differential was just not large enough to compensate investors for the impending capital losses. Sooner or later they were bound to realize this, and the dollar would then plunge.

In late 1986 the dollar was still well above the level that would balance

12. Krugman, "Is the Strong Dollar Sustainable?"

the current account. In contrast to the situation in early 1985, there was essentially no difference between real interest rates in the United States and in other industrial countries. Thus investors holding U.S. securities still faced the prospect of capital losses for which they would not receive compensating returns. They appear to have realized this, and the dollar fell again in early 1987.

ANNEX

Evidence from Comparative Model Simulations

THIS ANNEX contains the results of comparative simulations and other material provided by the six modeling groups that participated in the workshop on the U.S. current-account imbalance held at the Brookings Institution in January 1987. The material is divided into seven sections (I–VII), each focusing on a different set of simulations or model-related data. Sections I through V present comparative simulation results for historical tracking exercises, sensitivity tests, the baseline projection (scenario A), and two policy scenarios (B and C). Sections II through V each begin with a brief description of the instructions the modeling groups were asked to follow in preparing these simulations. Section VI presents a list of key income, price, and exchange rate elasticity estimates (including an indication of lag structures) for each of the models.

The participating modeling groups included the DRI model of the U.S. economy (DRI), the World Econometric Model of the Japanese Economic Planning Agency (EPA), the Multicountry Model of the Federal Reserve Board staff (MCM), the Global Economic Model of the National Institute of Economic and Social Research in London (NIESR GEM), the Interlink Model System of the OECD's Economic and Statistics Department (OECD), and the multicountry model of John Taylor (TAYLOR).[1]

In order to compare current-account simulations, we asked the modeling groups to disengage the U.S. current-account sectors from

1. The International Model of Wharton Econometric Associates (WHARTON) also ran the sensitivity tests and the baseline projection. Those results can be found in "Workshop on the U.S. Current-Account Imbalance: Model Memoranda for Federal Reserve MCM, OECD, WHARTON," Brookings Discussion Paper in International Economics 59-B, March 1987. The results do not appear in this Annex because they are not fully comparable with the results of the other models.

their larger multicountry models. This meant treating the key forcing variables (such as income, domestic prices, capacity utilization, and interest rates) as fixed or exogenous variables in the simulations.

Because of differences in model specifications, this separation of the current-account sector from the rest of the model could not be done uniformly. An effort was made by the workshop organizers, when they designed the various simulations, to deal with key specification differences among the models. For example, models that specify import demand as a function of GNP were given slightly different instructions from models that specify import equations as a function of total domestic demand. Models that specify import demand as a function of industrial production received still a third, slightly different set of instructions. In some cases, however, differences among the models may not have been handled adequately. As a result, the simulations may be less than fully comparable.

Section VII of this Annex presents a brief analysis of many of the key differences in structures and parameters across the participating models and notes how these differences affect the comparative sensitivity test results. The sensitivity tests were designed in part to help the interested reader understand the differences across models for the other simulations. A brief discussion of the historical tracking results and the forward-looking base case projection and policy simulations is contained in chapter 3. A more in-depth analysis of the historical tracking properties of one of the participating models, the MCM U.S. current-account sector, is given in chapter 2.

Historical Tracking

Table I-1. *Total U.S. Merchandise Exports, 1980–86: Historical Tracking Errors for Full-Block Solutions*
Percent error[a]

Model	1980	1981	1982	1983	1984	1985	1986[b]
				Volume			
DRI	−4.75	−1.87	0.68	0.17	−1.12	−0.63	1.94
EPA[c]	−1.69	1.66	1.72	1.62	0.35	2.38	7.64
MCM	−1.94	−0.99	1.53	0.03	−2.39	−0.34	2.71
NIESR GEM	−4.88	−1.04	−1.02	0.16	−2.08	0.12	1.05
OECD	−2.1	3.5	3.7	−0.6	−2.6	−2.9	n.a.
TAYLOR[d]	−3.79	−5.53	0.97	4.27	−1.08	2.02	3.79
				Price deflator			
DRI	−0.27	−0.14	0.89	0.65	0.09	1.12	3.63
EPA[c]	0.68	−1.02	−1.97	−2.63	−3.00	−3.23	−2.02
MCM	−0.21	−0.30	1.00	−0.81	−2.68	−1.24	1.70
NIESR GEM	1.32	−1.98	−2.93	−3.25	−3.45	−4.11	−6.00
OECD	2.0	−1.4	−3.4	−2.1	−3.8	−4.4	n.a.
TAYLOR[d]	−1.06	−0.56	2.52	4.11	4.50	7.92	12.42
				Value			
DRI	−4.99	−2.01	1.55	0.80	−1.02	0.47	5.66
EPA[c]	−0.95	0.65	−0.31	−1.06	−2.65	−0.92	7.11
MCM	−2.15	−1.25	2.58	−0.76	−5.01	−1.64	4.50
NIESR GEM	−3.62	−3.00	−3.92	−2.87	−5.26	−3.51	−4.32
OECD	−0.1	2.1	0.2	−2.7	−6.3	−7.2	n.a.
TAYLOR[d]	−4.81	−6.06	3.52	8.55	3.37	10.10	16.68

n.a. Not available.

a. Predicted minus actual as percentage of actual. Overprediction: +, underprediction: −.

b. First half of 1986 at an annual rate for MCM and NIESR GEM. First three quarters of 1986 at an annual rate for DRI and TAYLOR.

c. Data are from EPA solutions with exchange rate held exogenous.

d. TAYLOR model results are for goods and services rather than merchandise alone and are therefore not fully comparable with the results from the other models.

Table I-2. *Total U.S. Merchandise Imports, 1980–86: Historical Tracking Errors for Full-Block Solutions*

Percent error[a]

Model	1980	1981	1982	1983	1984	1985	1986[b]
				Volume			
DRI	1.05	−1.85	1.18	0.14	−4.31	−1.34	−5.89
EPA[c]	−0.94	−2.57	4.23	0.88	−0.91	−1.35	5.87
MCM	−0.74	1.01	0.88	1.30	−2.94	0.52	−2.28
NIESR GEM	−1.46	−1.58	−0.91	−2.36	−2.03	3.92	0.26
OECD	3.3	4.1	4.3	4.6	2.3	5.3	n.a.
TAYLOR[d]	3.90	4.83	4.80	3.08	−0.02	7.02	1.83
				Price deflator			
DRI	−0.43	0.47	−0.28	0.19	0.97	2.01	7.72
EPA[c]	0.00	0.00	0.00	0.00	0.00	0.00	0.00
MCM	0.31	1.75	0.10	−0.83	0.31	−0.11	3.14
NIESR GEM	−1.64	−1.83	−1.80	−0.55	−2.70	−2.70	−1.73
OECD	−2.2	−4.2	−7.9	−10.1	−14.6	−15.8	n.a.
TAYLOR[d]	−6.34	−5.52	−2.47	0.31	−0.63	−0.23	10.16
				Value			
DRI	0.60	−1.38	0.89	0.35	−3.38	0.68	1.48
EPA[c]	−0.90	−2.56	4.23	0.88	−0.92	−1.35	−5.88
MCM	−0.45	2.78	0.90	0.50	−2.57	0.49	0.80
NIESR GEM	−3.43	−3.86	−3.00	−1.12	−4.63	0.50	−1.96
OECD	1.0	−0.3	−3.9	−6.0	−12.6	−11.3	n.a.
TAYLOR[d]	−2.61	−0.94	2.21	3.42	−0.67	6.78	12.26

n.a. Not available.

a. Predicted minus actual as percentage of actual. Overprediction: +, underprediction: −.

b. First half of 1986 at an annual rate for MCM and NIESR GEM. First three quarters of 1986 at an annual rate for DRI and TAYLOR.

c. Data are from EPA solutions with exchange rate held exogenous.

d. TAYLOR model results are for goods and services rather than merchandise alone and are therefore not fully comparable with the results from the other models.

Figure I-1. *Actual and Predicted U.S. Trade Balance, 1980–86*

Billions of dollars

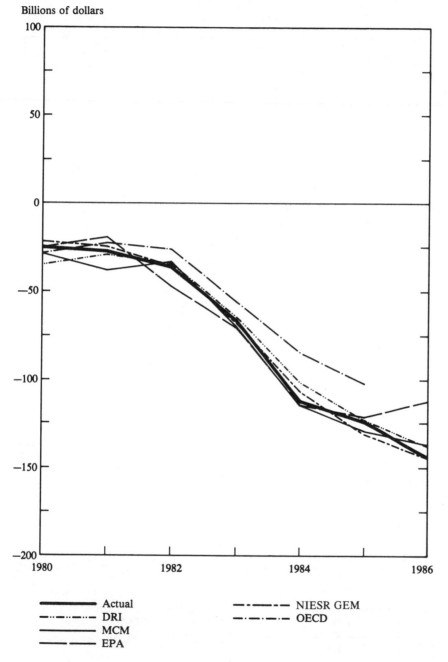

Actual ——— NIESR GEM —··—··—

DRI —···—···— OECD —··—··—

MCM ———

EPA ——— ———

Figure I-2. *Actual and Predicted U.S. Current-Account Balance,*
1979–86

Billions of dollars

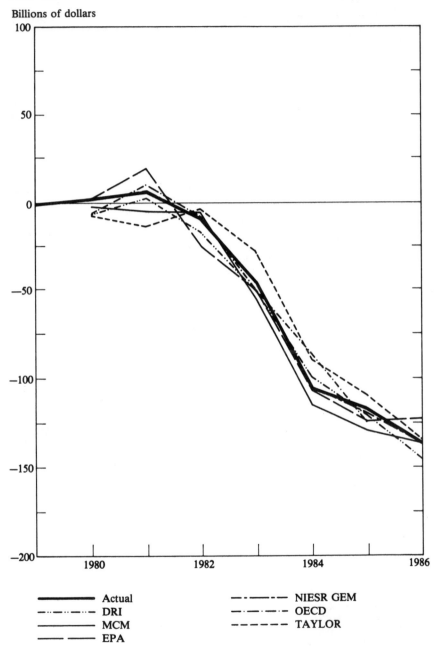

	Actual		NIESR GEM
	DRI		OECD
	MCM		TAYLOR
	EPA		

Table I-3. *U.S. Merchandise Trade Balance, 1980–86: Historical Tracking Errors for Full-Block Solutions*
Billions of dollars unless otherwise specified

Model	1980	1981	1982	1983	1984	1985	1986[a]
	Error in predicted level[b]						
DRI	−13	−1	1	1	9	−1	7
EPA[c]	0	8	−11	−4	−2	3	32
MCM	−4	−10	3	−3	−2	−5	7
NIESR GEM	3	3	0	−1	6	−7	−1
OECD	−3	−5	10	11	28	22	n.a.
Memorandum: Actual trade balance							
Balance of payments basis	−25.5	−28.0	−36.4	−67.1	−112.5	−124.4	−144.3
National income accounts basis	−22.4	−28.2	−35.5	−65.2	−110.3	−122.1	−145.4
	Error in predicted ratio of trade balance to GNP[d]						
DRI	−0.5	−0.0	0.0	0.0	0.2	−0.0	0.2
EPA[c]	0.0	0.3	−0.4	−0.1	−0.0	0.1	0.8
MCM	−0.1	−0.3	0.1	−0.1	−0.1	−0.1	0.1
NIESR GEM	0.1	0.1	0.0	−0.0	0.2	−0.2	−0.0
OECD	−0.1	0.2	0.3	0.3	0.7	0.6	n.a.
Memorandum: Actual ratio of trade balance to GNP (percent)							
Balance of payments basis	−0.93	−0.92	−1.15	−1.97	−2.99	−3.11	−3.47
National income accounts basis	−0.82	−0.92	−1.12	−1.92	−2.93	−3.05	−3.47

n.a. Not available.

a. First half of 1986 at an annual rate for MCM, NIESR GEM, and actual data. First three quarters of 1986 at an annual rate for DRI and TAYLOR.

b. Predicted level minus actual level in billions of dollars.

c. Data are from EPA solutions with exchange rate held exogenous.

d. Predicted ratio minus actual ratio in percentage points.

Table I-4. *U.S. Current-Account Balance, 1980–86: Historical Tracking Errors for Full-Block Solutions*
Billions of dollars unless otherwise specified

Model	1980	1981	1982	1983	1984	1985	1986[a]
				Error in predicted level[b]			
DRI	−8	−4	−8	−5	7	−4	−7
EPA[c]	0	13	−16	−5	−1	−7	14
MCM	−4	−11	4	−10	−9	−12	−0
NIESR GEM[d]	0	1	−0	−1	1	−2	−0
OECD	−8	4	1	−5	19	−8	n.a.
TAYLOR[e]	−9	−20	5	18	16	8	4
Memorandum: Actual current-account balance	1.9	6.3	−9.1	−46.6	−106.5	−117.5	−136.9
			Error in predicted ratio of current balance to GNP[f]				
DRI	−0.3	−0.1	−0.3	−0.2	0.2	−0.1	−0.2
EPA[c]	0.0	0.4	−0.5	−0.2	−0.0	−0.2	0.3
MCM	−0.2	−0.4	0.1	−0.3	−0.2	−0.3	−0.0
NIESR GEM[d]	0.0	0.0	−0.0	−0.0	0.0	−0.1	−0.0
OECD	−0.3	0.1	0.0	−0.1	0.5	−0.2	n.a.
TAYLOR[e]	−0.3	−0.7	0.2	0.5	0.4	0.2	0.1
Memorandum: Actual ratio of current balance to GNP (percent)	0.06	0.21	−0.29	−1.37	−2.83	−2.94	−3.29

n.a. Not available.

a. First half of 1986 at an annual rate for MCM, NIESR GEM, and actual data. First three quarters of 1986 at an annual rate for DRI and TAYLOR.

b. Predicted level minus actual level in billions of dollars.

c. Data are from EPA solutions with exchange rate held exogenous.

d. NIESR GEM model takes services and other nonmerchandise components of the current account as exogenous.

e. TAYLOR model results are for goods and services rather than entire current account and are therefore not fully comparable with the results from the other models.

f. Predicted ratio minus actual ratio in percentage points.

Sensitivity Tests

MODELING GROUPS were asked to run the following shocks relative to a baseline (scenario A, described in section III below):

One percent a year slower U.S. growth, over the whole prospective period, of all components of domestic demand. Models that did not disaggregate the "activity" variables in import equations were asked to set aggregate real GNP growing 1 percent slower than the baseline (2 instead of 3 percent) or, if U.S. industrial production was the activity variable, industrial production growing 1.5 percent slower (1.5 instead of 3 percent). Modeling groups were also asked to assume that manufacturing capacity grew at a rate 1.25 percent slower than in the base case and hence that capacity utilization declined at roughly 0.75 percent a year (relative to the unchanged capacity utilization rates in the base case).

One percent a year faster foreign growth, over the whole simulation period, of real GDP/GNP (components of domestic demand in *all* countries in the system other than the United States were assumed to grow faster by 1 percent a year). If foreign industrial production was used as the activity variable, modeling groups were asked to assume that the foreign regions experienced 1.5 percent faster growth (for example, Europe at 4.5 instead of 3 percent, Japan at 5 instead of 3.5 percent). If, but only if, these assumptions about foreign real growth proved operationally difficult to implement, modeling groups were asked to roughly approximate the shock by having all components of world trade grow faster by 2.5 percent a year. Analogous to the preceding shock, foreign capacity in manufacturing was assumed to grow 1.25 percent faster than on the baseline and hence that capacity utilization rates increased at roughly 0.75 percent a year.

Lower U.S. interest rates: All U.S. nominal interest rates (long and short) were reduced by two hundred basis points throughout the simulation period. (No change in foreign interest rates from their base case paths.)

Lower U.S. inflation: U.S. domestic prices (output prices if available,

109

otherwise GNP deflator) were assumed to grow more slowly, by 1 percent a year, over the whole simulation period.

Dollar depreciation (all currencies): The exchange value of the U.S. dollar was assumed to depreciate by 20 percent on January 1, 1986, in nominal terms and to remain 20 percent below scenario A throughout the rest of the simulation period. (The foreign currency price of the dollar, for every foreign currency, was assumed to fall by 20 percent— that is, a 25 percent rise in the U.S. dollar price of foreign currencies.)

Dollar depreciation (EMS and yen only): The U.S. dollar was assumed to depreciate by 20 percent on January 1, 1986, as above, but only against the EMS currencies and yen; all other foreign currencies, including the Canadian dollar, remained unchanged against the dollar from their scenario A paths.

Table II-1. *Effects of 1 Percent Slower U.S. Growth*
Percent deviation from baseline unless otherwise specified

Model	1986	1987	1988	1989	1990	1991
A. Effect on U.S. current account as percent of baseline GNP						
DRI	0.05	0.16	0.29	0.43	0.59	0.75
EPA	0.01	0.12	0.30	0.49	0.68	0.89
MCM[a]	0.03	0.24	0.49	0.77	1.07	1.39
NIESR GEM	0.09	0.22	0.31	0.40	0.52	0.66
OECD	0.13	0.32	0.52	0.73	0.95	1.18
TAYLOR	0.04	0.20	0.50	0.82	1.14	1.47
B. Effect on U.S. merchandise trade balance as percent of baseline GNP						
DRI	0.04	0.14	0.24	0.34	0.46	0.58
EPA	0.01	0.11	0.27	0.44	0.62	0.80
MCM[a]	0.02	0.20	0.40	0.61	0.84	1.07
NIESR GEM	0.09	0.22	0.31	0.40	0.52	0.66
OECD	0.11	0.28	0.44	0.61	0.78	0.95
TAYLOR	n.a.	n.a.	n.a.	n.a.	n.a.	n.a.
C. Effect on U.S. merchandise import volume						
DRI	−0.4	−1.5	−2.5	−3.5	−4.5	−5.5
EPA	−0.1	−1.3	−3.1	−4.9	−6.7	−8.5
MCM[a]	−0.3	−2.3	−4.3	−6.3	−8.2	−10.1
NIESR GEM	−1.0	−2.6	−4.2	−5.8	−7.4	−9.0
OECD	−1.1	−2.6	−4.2	−5.8	−7.4	−9.0
TAYLOR[b]	−0.4	−1.7	−4.0	−6.3	−8.5	−10.7

n.a. Not available.

a. For the tables in section II of the Annex only, the MCM simulations use an updated baseline simulation prepared in February 1987 following the January workshop. That February baseline incorporates additional historical data for 1986 that were unavailable in December 1986, when the original MCM baseline was prepared. The revised baseline shows smaller growth in export volumes, greater growth in import volumes, and larger deficits (in both constant-dollar and value terms). For details of the February baseline, see "Workshop on the U.S. Current-Account Imbalance: Model Memoranda for Federal Reserve MCM, OECD, WHARTON," Brookings Discussion Paper in International Economics 59-B, March 1987. Use of the February baseline for the calculations in these section II tables does not significantly influence the size of the estimated partial effects.

b. Imports of goods and services.

Table II-2. *Effects of 1 Percent Higher Foreign Growth*
Percent deviation from baseline unless otherwise specified

Model	1986	1987	1988	1989	1990	1991
A. *Effect on U.S. current account as percent of baseline GNP*						
DRI	0.07	0.21	0.37	0.55	0.74	0.94
EPA	0.01	0.08	0.16	0.24	0.33	0.42
MCM[a]	0.03	0.23	0.50	0.79	1.12	1.49
NIESR GEM	0.03	0.09	0.17	0.24	0.34	0.44
OECD	0.05	0.13	0.23	0.34	0.65	0.58
TAYLOR	0.01	0.04	0.14	0.26	0.40	0.54
B. *Effect on U.S. merchandise trade balance as percent of baseline GNP*						
DRI	0.03	0.12	0.22	0.31	0.41	0.51
EPA	0.01	0.08	0.15	0.23	0.31	0.39
MCM[a]	0.02	0.16	0.33	0.52	0.73	0.95
NIESR GEM	0.03	0.09	0.17	0.24	0.34	0.44
OECD	0.03	0.10	0.18	0.25	0.32	0.40
TAYLOR	n.a.	n.a.	n.a.	n.a.	n.a.	n.a.
C. *Effect on U.S. merchandise export volume*						
DRI	0.7	2.3	3.9	5.5	7.1	8.8
EPA	0.2	1.4	2.6	3.8	5.0	6.3
MCM[a]	0.4	2.4	4.7	6.9	9.1	11.4
NIESR GEM	0.6	2.0	3.4	5.0	6.2	8.2
OECD	0.6	1.6	2.8	4.0	5.3	6.6
TAYLOR[b]	0.1	0.5	1.4	2.6	3.8	5.1

n.a. Not available.
a. See note a to Annex table II-1.
b. Exports of real goods and services.

Table II-3. *Effect of a 2 Percentage Point Decline in U.S. Interest Rates*
Deviation from baseline

Model	1986	1987	1988	1989	1990	1991
A. *Effect on U.S. current account as percent of baseline GNP*						
DRI	0.06	0.14	0.18	0.21	0.23	0.25
EPA	0.04	0.27	0.32	0.34	0.36	0.37
EPA-II[a]	0.07	0.66	1.37	1.45	1.44	1.53
MCM[b]	0.00	0.05	0.11	0.15	0.20	0.24
NIESR GEM	n.a.	n.a.	n.a.	n.a.	n.a.	n.a.
OECD	0.00	0.06	0.11	0.16	0.18	0.22
TAYLOR	−0.06	−0.08	−0.02	0.05	0.10	0.13

n.a. Not available.
a. Data are from EPA solution with exchange rate determined endogenously.
b. See note a to Annex table II-1.

Table II-4. *Effects of a 1 Percentage Point Decline in U.S. Inflation*
Percent deviation from baseline unless otherwise specified

Model	1986	1987	1988	1989	1990	1991
A. *Effect on U.S. current account as percent of baseline GNP*						
DRI	−0.02	0.03	0.11	0.20	0.30	0.42
EPA	−0.00	0.04	0.13	0.23	0.34	0.46
MCM[a]	0.00	0.03	0.11	0.23	0.36	0.50
NIESR GEM	0.02	0.04	0.10	0.18	0.27	0.36
OECD	−0.01	0.01	0.05	0.10	0.17	0.23
TAYLOR	−0.01	0.00	0.03	0.07	0.12	0.17
B. *Effect on U.S. merchandise export prices*						
DRI	−0.58	−1.56	−2.52	−3.49	−4.47	−5.45
EPA	−0.20	−1.19	−2.23	−3.27	−4.29	−5.30
MCM[a]	−0.17	−1.02	−1.96	−2.88	−3.77	−4.67
NIESR GEM	−0.30	−1.10	−1.80	−2.60	−3.30	−4.10
OECD	−0.42	−1.06	−1.69	−2.34	−2.98	−3.61
TAYLOR[b]	−0.2	−0.8	−1.8	−2.8	−3.7	−4.6
C. *Effect on U.S. merchandise import prices*						
DRI	−0.02	−0.10	−0.21	−0.31	−0.41	−0.50
EPA	0.00	0.00	0.00	0.00	0.00	0.00
MCM[a]	0.00	0.00	0.00	0.00	0.00	0.00
NIESR GEM	−0.30	−0.9	−1.50	−2.00	−2.50	−3.10
OECD	−0.01	−0.1	−0.1	−0.2	−0.2	−0.3
TAYLOR[c]	0.00	0.00	0.00	0.00	0.00	0.00
D. *Effect on U.S. merchandise import volumes*						
DRI	−0.12	−0.75	−1.48	−2.22	−2.96	−3.72
EPA	−0.07	−0.77	−1.86	−2.96	−4.07	−5.17
MCM[a]	−0.08	−0.76	−1.69	−2.65	−3.60	−4.55
NIESR GEM	0.00	−0.20	−0.70	−1.60	−2.40	−3.20
OECD	−0.08	−0.40	−0.80	−1.23	−1.67	−2.11
TAYLOR	−0.1	−0.5	−1.1	−1.7	−2.3	−2.9
E. *Effect on U.S. merchandise export volumes*						
DRI	0.07	0.61	1.40	2.25	3.14	4.05
EPA	0.06	0.61	1.44	2.35	3.28	4.22
MCM[a]	0.00	0.19	0.88	1.78	2.67	3.57
NIESR GEM	0.00	0.30	0.80	1.30	1.90	2.50
OECD	0.21	0.57	1.10	1.73	2.40	3.08
TAYLOR	0.00	0.2	0.7	1.3	1.9	2.5

a. See note a to Annex table II-1.
b. Deflator for exports of goods and services.
c. Deflator for imports of goods and services.

Table II-5. *Effects of a 20 Percent Dollar Depreciation against All Other Currencies*

Percent deviation from baseline unless otherwise specified

Model	1986	1987	1988	1989	1990	1991
A. Effect on U.S. current account as percent of baseline GNP						
DRI	−0.34	0.87	1.57	1.75	1.94	2.08
EPA	−0.23	0.92	1.35	1.44	1.48	1.51
MCM[a]	0.11	1.43	2.18	2.35	2.55	2.73
NIESR GEM	−0.19	0.29	1.29	1.41	1.39	1.38
OECD	−0.92	0.35	1.06	1.19	1.25	1.30
TAYLOR[b]	0.00	−0.18	−0.13	0.02	0.16	0.26
B. Effect on U.S. merchandise trade balance as percent of baseline GNP						
DRI	−0.39	0.65	1.19	1.23	1.26	1.29
EPA	−0.22	0.84	1.23	1.30	1.33	1.36
MCM[a]	−0.03	1.14	1.74	1.80	1.88	1.95
NIESR GEM	−0.19	0.29	1.29	1.41	1.39	1.38
OECD	−1.04	0.00	0.66	0.73	0.74	0.74
TAYLOR	n.a.	n.a.	n.a.	n.a.	n.a.	n.a.
C. Effect on real net exports of goods and services as percent of baseline real GNP						
DRI	0.75	2.77	3.57	3.86	4.18	4.47
EPA	0.00	2.68	4.03	4.42	4.73	5.00
MCM[a]	1.31	3.61	4.58	4.87	5.13	5.33
NIESR GEM	0.23	0.74	1.85	2.05	2.07	2.11
OECD	1.37	2.61	3.29	3.50	3.64	3.73
TAYLOR[b]	0.00	0.50	1.39	2.14	2.74	3.19
D. Effect on merchandise import volume						
DRI	−2.8	−11.2	−14.6	−15.1	−15.3	−15.7
EPA	−3.6	−16.8	−18.9	−19.0	−19.1	−19.2
MCM	−6.9	−17.3	−20.2	−20.6	−20.9	−20.9
NIESR GEM	−0.6	−1.9	−12.0	−14.5	−14.7	−14.8
OECD	−5.9	−10.8	−13.4	−14.6	−15.1	−15.2
TAYLOR[b,c]	0.0	−2.6	−6.4	−9.0	−10.6	−11.6
E. Effect on merchandise export volume						
DRI	4.2	15.4	17.7	17.6	17.7	17.8
EPA	2.5	10.0	12.3	12.8	12.8	12.8
MCM	2.6	13.5	18.0	17.6	17.5	17.4
NIESR GEM	3.2	10.7	13.7	12.7	11.7	10.8
OECD	5.1	9.5	11.5	11.2	11.2	11.3
TAYLOR[b,d]	0.0	1.3	4.4	7.5	9.9	11.7

Continued on next page

Table II-5 *(continued)*

Model	1986	1987	1988	1989	1990	1991
F. Effect on merchandise import prices						
DRI	11.6	18.9	18.7	18.8	19.0	19.3
EPA	10.3	20.0	20.0	20.0	20.0	20.0
MCM	11.5	20.8	21.9	22.4	22.6	22.4
NIESR GEM	4.8	5.5	5.6	5.8	6.0	6.2
OECD	23.5	25.0	25.0	25.0	25.0	25.0
TAYLOR[b,c]	0.0	5.3	11.7	16.2	19.2	21.2
G. Effect on merchandise export prices						
DRI	2.4	3.9	4.0	3.9	3.9	3.9
EPA	2.2	4.1	4.1	4.1	4.1	4.1
MCM	3.2	5.6	5.7	5.7	5.7	5.7
NIESR GEM	0.0	0.0	0.0	0.0	0.0	0.0
OECD	4.7	8.0	8.4	8.5	8.0	7.8
TAYLOR[b,d]	0.0	0.0	0.0	0.0	0.0	0.0

n.a. Not available.
a. See note a to Annex table II-1.
b. Exchange value of U.S. dollar depreciates on January 1, 1987, rather than January 1, 1986.
c. Imports of goods and services.
d. Exports of goods and services.

Table II-6. *Effects of a 20 Percent Dollar Depreciation against the Yen and EMS Currencies*

Percent deviation from baseline unless specified otherwise

Model	1986	1987	1988	1989	1990	1991
A. Effect on U.S. current account as percent of baseline GNP						
DRI	−0.19	0.51	0.92	1.02	1.13	1.21
EPA	−0.07	0.38	0.56	0.59	0.61	0.63
MCM[a]	0.12	0.92	1.39	1.49	1.62	1.75
NIESR GEM	−0.09	0.22	0.87	1.00	1.02	1.05
OECD	−0.72	0.00	0.52	0.60	0.63	0.65
TAYLOR[b]	0.00	−0.13	−0.10	0.01	0.11	0.19
B. Effect on U.S. merchandise trade balance as percent of baseline GNP						
DRI	−0.22	0.38	0.69	0.72	0.73	0.75
EPA	−0.05	0.33	0.48	0.50	0.52	0.53
MCM[a]	0.06	0.77	1.14	1.18	1.24	1.29
NIESR GEM	−0.09	0.22	0.87	1.00	1.02	1.05
OECD	−0.77	−0.15	0.30	0.35	0.35	0.35
TAYLOR	n.a.	n.a.	n.a.	n.a.	n.a.	n.a.

Table II-6 (continued)

Model	1986	1987	1988	1989	1990	1991
C. Effect on real net exports of goods and services as percent of baseline real GNP						
DRI	0.45	1.66	2.15	2.32	2.51	2.68
EPA	0.00	1.07	1.81	1.96	2.02	2.09
MCM[a]	0.70	2.09	2.70	2.89	3.07	3.19
NIESR GEM	0.14	0.54	1.08	1.43	1.51	1.59
OECD	0.94	1.77	2.25	2.41	2.50	2.55
TAYLOR[b]	0.00	0.37	1.05	1.61	2.06	2.40
D. Effect on merchandise import volume						
DRI	−1.6	−6.8	−8.9	−9.2	−9.4	−9.6
EPA	−1.4	−6.7	−7.7	−7.8	−7.8	−7.8
MCM	−3.5	−9.6	−11.5	−11.9	−12.2	−12.2
NIESR GEM	−0.3	−0.9	−7.4	−9.8	−10.4	−10.9
OECD	−4.6	−8.6	−10.7	−11.8	−12.2	−12.2
TAYLOR[b,c]	0.0	−1.9	−4.9	−6.8	−8.1	−8.9
E. Effect on merchandise export volume						
DRI	2.5	9.0	10.3	10.3	10.3	10.4
EPA	0.7	3.0	3.7	3.9	3.9	3.9
MCM	1.8	9.0	11.8	11.5	11.4	11.4
NIESR GEM	2.2	7.8	10.3	9.8	9.3	8.8
OECD	2.7	4.8	5.8	5.5	5.5	5.5
TAYLOR[b,d]	0.0	1.0	3.3	5.6	7.4	8.6
F. Effect on merchandise import prices						
DRI	6.6	10.6	10.6	10.6	10.7	10.9
EPA	3.5	6.9	6.9	6.9	6.9	6.9
MCM	5.5	10.7	11.4	11.9	12.0	11.9
NIESR GEM	2.8	3.5	3.8	4.0	4.3	4.7
OECD	16.8	18.6	19.3	19.3	19.3	19.3
TAYLOR[b,c]	0.0	3.9	8.7	11.9	14.0	15.5
G. Effect on merchandise export prices						
DRI	1.4	2.3	2.3	2.3	2.3	2.3
EPA	1.3	2.3	2.3	2.3	2.3	2.3
MCM	2.4	4.3	4.5	4.5	4.5	4.5
NIESR GEM	0.0	0.0	0.0	0.0	0.0	0.0
OECD	3.5	6.0	6.7	6.4	6.1	6.0
TAYLOR[b,d]	0.0	0.0	0.0	0.0	0.0	0.0

n.a. Not available.

a. See note a to Annex table II-1.

b. Exchange value of U.S. dollar depreciates on January 1, 1987, rather than January 1, 1986.

c. Imports of goods and services.

d. Exports of goods and services.

Scenario A: Base Case

THE MAIN instructions used in constructing the baseline projection were:[1]

U.S. real GNP, industrial production, potential output, and manufacturing capacity were assumed to grow at a constant 3 percent annual rate from the third quarter of 1986.

U.S. GNP deflator and unit labor costs were assumed to grow at a constant 3.5 percent annual rate from the third quarter of 1986.

Nominal U.S. interest rates were assumed to remain constant beginning in the fourth quarter of 1986 through the end of 1991 (three-month Treasury bills, 5.5 percent; federal funds, 6 percent; long-term U.S. government bonds, 8 percent).

Foreign real GNPs, potential outputs, and manufacturing capacities were assumed to grow at constant annual rates from the third quarter of 1986 (Canada, 3 percent; Japan, 3.5 percent; Europe, 3 percent).

Bilateral exchange rates between foreign currencies and the U.S. dollar were assumed to remain constant in real terms at the average values prevailing in the third quarter of 1986 (with GNP deflators used to translate nominal to real exchange rates).

Oil prices were assumed to remain constant in real terms at $16 a barrel from the fourth quarter of 1986.

1. For further details see the memorandum dated October 21, 1986, in "Workshop on the U.S. Current-Account Imbalance: Comparative Tables and Charts," Brookings Discussion Paper in International Economics 58, March 1987.

Table III-1. *Scenario A: U.S. Current-Account Balance*

Billions of dollars unless otherwise specified

Model	1986	1987	1988	1989	1990	1991
			Projected level			
DRI	−141	−129	−133	−150	−172	−198
EPA	−127	−133	−147	−168	−192	−219
MCM	−143	−125	−120	−133	−150	−167
NIESR GEM	−123	−127	−69	−48	−56	−60
OECD	n.a.	n.a.	n.a.	n.a.	n.a.	n.a.
TAYLOR	−153[a]	−162	−181	−207	−239	−280
		Ratio to nominal GNP (percentage points)				
DRI	−3.3	−2.9	−2.8	−3.0	−3.2	−3.4
EPA	−3.0	−3.0	−3.1	−3.3	−3.5	−3.8
MCM	−3.4	−2.8	−2.5	−2.6	−2.8	−2.9
NIESR GEM	−2.9	−2.8	−1.4	−0.9	−1.0	−1.0
OECD	n.a.	n.a.	n.a.	n.a.	n.a.	n.a.
TAYLOR[b]	−3.5[a]	−3.6	−3.8	−4.1	−4.4	−4.8

n.a. Not available.
a. Figure refers to 1986:4 only.
b. Figures calculated by averaging the quarterly ratios.

Table III-2. *Scenario A: Real Net Exports of U.S. Goods and Services*[a]

Billions of 1982 dollars unless otherwise specified

Model	1986	1987	1988	1989	1990	1991
			Projected level			
DRI	−146	−111	−112	−122	−136	−152
EPA	−112	−109	−119	−135	−153	−173
MCM	−144	−111	−111	−133	−156	−174
NIESR GEM	−146	−136	−77	−59	−64	−68
OECD	n.a.	n.a.	n.a.	n.a.	n.a.	n.a.
TAYLOR	−149[b]	−125	−101	−90	−90	−100
		Ratio to constant-dollar GNP (percentage points)				
DRI	−4.0	−2.9	−2.9	−3.0	−3.3	−3.6
EPA	−3.1	−2.9	−3.1	−3.4	−3.7	−4.1
MCM	−3.9	−2.9	−2.8	−3.3	−3.8	−4.1
NIESR GEM	−4.0	−3.6	−2.0	−1.5	−1.6	−1.6
OECD	n.a.	n.a.	n.a.	n.a.	n.a.	n.a.
TAYLOR	−4.0[b]	−3.3	−2.6	−2.2	−2.2	−2.3

n.a. Not available.
a. National income accounts basis.
b. Figure refers to 1986:4 only.

Figure III-1. *Scenario A: U.S. Current-Account Balance, Actual 1979–86 and Projected 1987–91*

Billions of dollars

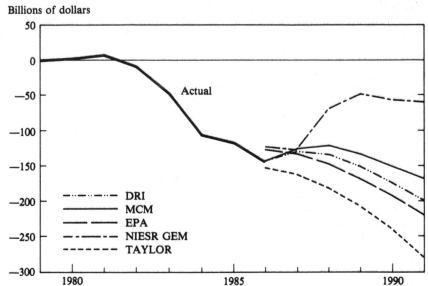

Figure III-2. *Scenario A: Real Net Exports of U.S. Goods and Services, Actual 1979–86 and Projected 1987–91*[a]

Billions of 1982 dollars

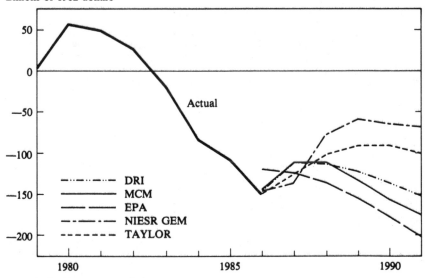

a. National income accounts basis.

Table III-3. *Scenario A: U.S. Merchandise Trade Balance*
Billions of dollars unless otherwise specified

Model	1986	1987	1988	1989	1990	1991
			Projected level			
DRI	− 147	− 137	− 145	− 165	− 190	− 217
EPA	− 117	− 122	− 133	− 150	− 170	− 192
MCM	− 146	− 122	− 114	− 124	− 136	− 148
NIESR GEM	− 139	− 136	− 84	− 63	− 67	− 72
OECD	n.a.	n.a.	n.a.	n.a.	n.a.	n.a.
TAYLOR	n.a.	n.a.	n.a.	n.a.	n.a.	n.a.
		Ratio to nominal GNP (percentage points)				
DRI	− 3.5	− 3.1	− 3.0	− 3.3	− 3.5	− 3.8
EPA	− 2.8	− 2.7	− 2.8	− 2.9	− 3.1	− 3.3
MCM	− 3.5	− 2.7	− 2.4	− 2.4	− 2.5	− 2.6
NIESR GEM	− 3.3	− 3.0	− 1.7	− 1.2	− 1.2	− 1.2
OECD	n.a.	n.a.	n.a.	n.a.	n.a.	n.a.
TAYLOR	n.a.	n.a.	n.a.	n.a.	n.a.	n.a.

n.a. Not available.

Table III-4. *Scenario A: Total U.S. Merchandise Exports*
Annual percent change

Model	1986	1987	1988	1989	1990	1991
			Volume			
DRI	4.3	14.5	8.0	5.9	6.0	6.1
EPA	7.1	6.4	5.5	4.3	4.2	4.2
MCM	6.6	18.7	11.7	6.3	6.1	6.1
NIESR GEM	3.7	14.0	9.7	7.1	7.0	7.8
OECD	n.a.	n.a.	n.a.	n.a.	n.a.	n.a.
TAYLOR[a]	n.a.	6.3	9.4	7.9	6.6	5.7
			Price deflator			
DRI	− 3.4	0.4	1.5	1.2	1.2	1.1
EPA	1.6	3.9	3.8	3.9	3.9	3.9
MCM	− 2.7	3.1	4.5	4.3	4.5	4.6
NIESR GEM	− 0.1	− 2.7	0.1	2.4	2.6	2.6
OECD	n.a.	n.a.	n.a.	n.a.	n.a.	n.a.
TAYLOR[a]	n.a.	2.6	4.1	4.0	3.9	3.9

n.a. Not available.
a. TAYLOR model equations are for goods and services combined rather than merchandise only. Growth rates for 1987 use 1986:4 as a base.

Table III-5. *Scenario A: Total U.S. Merchandise Imports*

Annual percent change

Model	1986	1987	1988	1989	1990	1991
			Volume			
DRI	12.6	0.9	6.2	7.1	7.6	7.5
EPA	5.6	5.3	6.3	6.6	6.6	6.6
MCM	13.3	1.9	6.8	8.1	7.9	6.8
NIESR GEM	13.1	5.6	−9.8	−0.5	6.3	7.5
OECD	n.a.	n.a.	n.a.	n.a.	n.a.	n.a.
TAYLOR[a]	n.a.	0.0	2.6	4.5	5.6	6.4
			Price deflator			
DRI	−4.3	5.3	2.0	2.3	2.2	2.2
EPA	−2.2	3.1	3.0	3.0	3.0	3.0
MCM	−4.1	4.9	2.5	2.0	2.6	3.3
NIESR GEM	−5.1	0.2	2.1	2.4	2.4	2.4
OECD	n.a.	n.a.	n.a.	n.a.	n.a.	n.a.
TAYLOR[a]	n.a.	8.5	11.1	8.3	6.6	5.5

n.a. Not available.

a. TAYLOR model equations are for goods and services combined rather than merchandise only. Growth rates for 1987 use 1986:4 as a base.

Scenario B: Change in U.S. Policy Mix

SCENARIO B postulated a reduction of the U.S. fiscal deficit and an acceleration in U.S. money supply growth relative to the baseline in scenario A, specifically, (a) a sustained reduction in U.S. government spending equivalent to 1 percent of baseline real GNP in 1988, accompanied by further reductions of two-thirds of a percent of baseline real GNP in 1989 and 1990, each sustained through 1991; plus (b) an expansion of money growth taking the form of a 2 percent higher growth *rate* in each of the years 1988–91 (leaving the level of the money stock roughly 2 percent above scenario A by the end of 1988, some 4 percent higher by the end of 1989, and so forth).

The main assumptions used in constructing the scenario were:[1]

For simplicity, the foreign variables appearing as right-hand-side determinants in equations for the U.S. current-account block were assumed to be unchanged from the paths followed in scenario A.

U.S. real GNP was assumed to grow at the following annual rates for the five years 1987–91: 3 percent, 2 percent, 2 percent, 2 percent, and 3 percent. This left the level of real GNP in 1991 some 3 percentage points less than its level in scenario A. The level of industrial production in the United States was assumed to be below the A path by some 5.25 percent by 1991. U.S. total domestic demand was assumed to grow during 1987–91 at 3 percent, 1.5 percent, 1.25 percent, 1.25 percent, and 2.25 percent (ending 5.75 percent below its A path). Growth in potential output was assumed to remain unchanged from its path in scenario A (constant 3 percent a year).

U.S. consumer price inflation was assumed to accelerate marginally

1. For further details see the memoranda dated October 21, 1986, and November 24, 1986, in "Workshop on the U.S. Current-Account Imbalance: Comparative Tables and Charts," Brookings Discussion Paper in International Economics 58, March 1987.

relative to scenario A, ending some half a percentage point faster in 1991. Annual inflation rates for 1987–91 were 3.5 percent, 3.6 percent, 3.8 percent, 3.9 percent, and 3.9 percent (relative to a constant 3.5 percent rate in scenario A).

U.S. interest rates: The federal funds rate was assumed to decline steadily over 1987–91 from an assumed level of 6 percent in 1987; long-term U.S. government bond yields were assumed to decline from 8 percent in 1987 to 5.5 percent in 1991.

The nominal value of the dollar was assumed to depreciate in exchange markets relative to its value in scenario A. Expressed as deviations from the scenario A baseline, a nominal index was assumed during the five years 1987–91 to fall by (annual averages) 0 percent, −3.3 percent, −6.6 percent, −10.1 percent, and −12.2 percent.

Table IV-1. *Scenario B: U.S. Current-Account Balance*

Billions of dollars unless otherwise specified

Model	1986	1987	1988	1989	1990	1991
	Projected deviation from scenario A					
DRI	0	0	5	24	51	80
EPA	0	0	7	26	49	73
MCM	0	−0	7	34	72	109
NIESR GEM	0	0	4	12	31	51
OECD	n.a.	n.a.	n.a.	n.a.	n.a.	n.a.
TAYLOR	0	−0	7	23	45	62
MCM, full-model simulation	0	0	11	29	51	68
TAYLOR, full-model simulation	n.a.	n.a.	n.a.	n.a.	n.a.	n.a.
	Ratio to nominal GNP, deviation from A ratio (percentage points)					
DRI	0.0	0.0	0.1	0.5	0.9	1.4
EPA	0.0	0.0	0.1	0.5	0.9	1.3
MCM	0.0	−0.0	0.1	0.6	1.3	1.9
NIESR GEM	0.0	0.0	0.0	0.2	0.5	0.8
OECD	n.a.	n.a.	n.a.	n.a.	n.a.	n.a.
TAYLOR	0.0	0.0	0.1	0.4	0.8	1.0
MCM, full-model simulation	0.0	0.0	0.2	0.5	0.9	1.2
TAYLOR, full-model simulation	0.0	0.0	−0.4	−0.6	−0.7	−0.8

n.a. Not available.

Table IV-2. *Scenario B: Real Net Exports of U.S. Goods and Services*[a]

Billions of 1982 dollars unless otherwise specified

Model	1986	1987	1988	1989	1990	1991
	Projected deviation from scenario A					
DRI	0	0	9	35	67	100
EPA	0	0	13	37	64	85
MCM	0	1	13	48	92	131
NIESR GEM	0	0	6	17	36	56
OECD	n.a.	n.a.	n.a.	n.a.	n.a.	n.a.
TAYLOR	0	0	9	30	57	81
MCM, full-model simulation	0	0	17	45	77	103
TAYLOR, full-model simulation	n.a.	n.a.	n.a.	n.a.	n.a.	n.a.
	Ratio to constant-dollar GNP, deviation from A ratio (percentage points)					
DRI	0.0	0.0	0.2	0.9	1.6	2.3
EPA	0.0	0.0	0.3	0.9	1.6	2.1
MCM	0.0	0.0	0.3	1.2	2.2	3.0
NIESR GEM	0.0	0.0	0.1	0.4	0.9	1.3
OECD	n.a.	n.a.	n.a.	n.a.	n.a.	n.a.
TAYLOR	0.0	0.2	0.2	0.7	1.4	1.9
MCM, full-model simulation	0.0	0.0	0.4	1.1	1.8	2.4
TAYLOR, full-model simulation	n.a.	n.a.	n.a.	n.a.	n.a.	n.a.

n.a. Not available.
a. National income accounts basis.

Figure IV-1. *Scenario B: U.S. Current-Account Balance, Actual 1979–86 and Projected 1987–91*

Billions of dollars

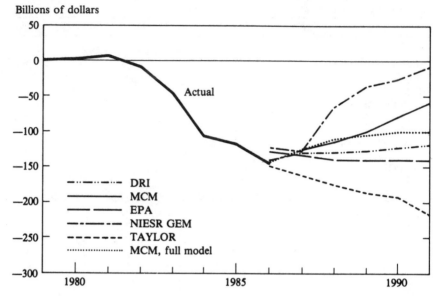

Figure IV-2. *Scenario B: Real Net Exports of U.S. Goods and Services, Actual 1979–86 and Projected 1987–91*[a]

Billions of 1982 dollars

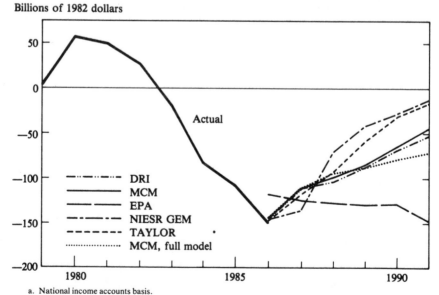

a. National income accounts basis.

Table IV-3. *Scenario B: Total U.S. Merchandise Exports*

Percent deviation from scenario A

Model	1986	1987	1988	1989	1990	1991
			Volume			
DRI	0.0	0.0	0.6	2.8	5.4	7.9
EPA	0.0	0.0	0.4	0.9	1.4	1.6
MCM	0.0	0.0	0.4	2.2	4.5	6.8
NIESR GEM	0.0	0.0	0.4	1.4	3.0	4.7
OECD	n.a.	n.a.	n.a.	n.a.	n.a.	n.a.
TAYLOR[a]	0.0	0.0	0.2	0.7	1.6	2.7
MCM, full-model simulation	0.0	0.0	−0.3	1.5	4.2	7.8
TAYLOR, full-model simulation[a]	0.0	0.0	44.9	102.1	103.1	80.4
			Price deflator			
DRI	0.0	0.0	0.3	1.0	1.8	2.5
EPA	0.0	0.0	0.4	0.9	1.6	2.2
MCM	0.0	−0.0	0.5	1.5	2.7	3.8
NIESR GEM	0.0	0.0	0.0	0.2	0.5	0.8
OECD	n.a.	n.a.	n.a.	n.a.	n.a.	n.a.
TAYLOR[a]	0.0	0.0	0.0	0.2	0.6	1.0
MCM, full-model simulation	0.0	0.0	0.4	1.0	1.7	2.4
TAYLOR, full-model simulation[a]	0.0	0.0	0.7	3.2	6.0	8.6

n.a. Not available.

a. TAYLOR model results are for goods and services rather than merchandise alone and are therefore not fully comparable with the results from the other models.

Table IV-4. *Scenario B: Total U.S. Merchandise Imports*
Percent deviation from scenario A

Model	1986	1987	1988	1989	1990	1991
Volume						
DRI	0.0	0.0	−0.7	−3.3	−6.6	−9.3
EPA	0.0	0.0	−1.3	−4.3	−7.2	−9.2
MCM	0.0	−0.0	−2.3	−7.3	−12.5	−16.2
NIESR GEM	0.0	0.0	−1.6	−3.8	−7.7	−10.9
OECD	n.a.	n.a.	n.a.	n.a.	n.a.	n.a.
TAYLOR[a]	0.0	0.0	−1.5	−4.6	−7.9	−10.1
MCM, full-model simulation	0.0	0.0	−3.5	−7.1	−10.1	−11.6
TAYLOR, full-model simulation[a]	0.0	0.0	63.2	109.1	81.3	62.3
Price deflator						
DRI	0.0	0.0	1.5	3.9	6.5	8.5
EPA	0.0	0.0	1.1	2.3	3.5	4.2
MCM	0.0	−0.0	1.8	5.0	8.7	11.9
NIESR GEM	0.0	0.0	0.8	1.8	3.1	4.2
OECD	n.a.	n.a.	n.a.	n.a.	n.a.	n.a.
TAYLOR[a]	0.0	0.0	0.7	2.4	4.6	6.9
MCM, full-model simulation	0.0	0.0	1.5	4.6	8.3	11.8
TAYLOR, full-model simulation[a]	0.0	0.0	2.6	5.6	7.9	9.9

n.a. Not available.
a. See note a to Annex table IV-3.

Scenario C: Change in U.S. Policy Mix Plus Expansionary Policies in Foreign Countries

SCENARIO C postulated changes in the policies of both the U.S. and foreign governments, specifically, the U.S. policy changes assumed for scenario B (see Annex section IV); an expansion in foreign governments' expenditures in 1987 equivalent to 1 percent of baseline (scenario A) real GNP, sustained thereafter through 1991; plus an acceleration in the rate of foreign monetary growth of 2 percentage points a year from 1987 through 1991.

The main assumptions used in constructing the scenario were:[1]

The nominal foreign exchange value of the dollar in scenario C was assumed to be higher than in scenario B but lower than in scenario A. Expressed as deviations from scenario A, the dollar was lower (in terms of annual averages) by 0 percent in 1987, -0.7 percent in 1988, -2.2 percent in 1989, -3.8 percent in 1990, and -4.2 percent in 1991. (Deviations from scenario B for 1987–91 were $+0.6$ percent, $+2.6$ percent, $+4.4$ percent, $+6.3$ percent, and $+8.0$ percent.)

In all foreign countries real GNP growth was assumed to be faster than in scenarios A and B. Expressed as deviations from scenarios A and B, foreign output in 1987–91 was higher by 1.6 percent, 2.0 percent, 2.5 percent, 2.75 percent, and 3.0 percent.

Inflation in foreign countries was assumed to be somewhat higher relative to scenarios A and B; GNP deflators were higher in 1987–91 (as a percentage of the baseline) by 0.3 percent, 1.4 percent, 2.1 percent, 3.3 percent, and 4.6 percent.

For simplicity, U.S. variables other than the exchange value of the dollar were assumed to take the same paths as in scenario B.

1. For further details see the memoranda dated October 21, 1986, and November 24, 1986, in "Workshop on the U.S. Current-Account Imbalance: Comparative Tables and Charts," Brookings Discussion Paper in International Economics 58, March 1987.

127

Table V-1. *Scenario C: U.S. Current-Account Balance*
Billions of dollars unless otherwise specified

Model	1986	1987	1988	1989	1990	1991
		Projected deviation from scenario A				
DRI	2	9	19	42	70	99
EPA	0	8	22	49	82	119
MCM	0	15	33	69	110	151
NIESR GEM	0	3	7	15	30	44
OECD	n.a.	n.a.	n.a.	n.a.	n.a.	n.a.
TAYLOR	0	4	17	39	66	87
MCM, full-model simulation	0	0	18	31	43	52
NIESR GEM, full-model simulation	0	1	6	-1	-14	-27
		Ratio to nominal GNP, deviation from A ratio (percentage points)				
DRI	0.0	0.2	0.4	0.8	1.3	1.7
EPA	0.0	0.2	0.5	1.0	1.5	2.1
MCM	0.0	0.3	0.7	1.3	2.0	2.6
NIESR GEM	0.0	0.0	0.1	0.3	0.5	0.7
OECD	n.a.	n.a.	n.a.	n.a.	n.a.	n.a.
TAYLOR	0.0	0.1	0.3	0.7	1.1	1.4
MCM, full-model simulation	0.0	0.0	0.4	0.6	0.8	0.9
NIESR GEM, full-model simulation	0.0	-0.0	0.1	-0.1	-0.3	-0.5

n.a. Not available.

Table V-2. *Scenario C: Real Net Exports of U.S. Goods
and Services*[a]

Billions of 1982 dollars unless otherwise specified

Model	1986	1987	1988	1989	1990	1991
		Projected deviation from scenario A				
DRI	0	8	20	45	76	105
EPA	0	8	28	57	91	125
MCM	0	18	42	82	124	164
NIESR GEM	0	2	7	16	31	35
OECD	n.a.	n.a,	n.a.	n.a.	n.a.	n.a.
TAYLOR	0	3	16	37	63	85
MCM, full-model simulation	0	0	21	40	58	72
NIESR GEM, full-model simulation	0	1	6	−1	−3	−25
		Ratio to constant-dollar GNP,				
		deviation from A ratio (percentage points)				
DRI	0.0	0.2	0.5	1.1	1.8	2.5
EPA	0.0	0.2	0.7	1.4	2.2	2.9
MCM	0.0	0.5	1.1	2.0	3.0	3.8
NIESR GEM	0.0	0.0	0.2	0.4	0.7	0.8
OECD	n.a.	n.a.	n.a.	n.a.	n.a.	n.a.
TAYLOR	0.0	0.1	0.4	0.9	1.5	2.0
MCM, full-model simulation	0.0	0.0	0.5	1.0	1.4	1.7
NIESR GEM, full-model simulation	0.0	0.0	0.1	−0.0	−0.1	−0.6

n.a. Not available.
a. National income accounts basis.

Figure V-1. *Scenario C: U.S. Current-Account Balance, Actual 1979–86 and Projected 1987–91*

Billions of dollars

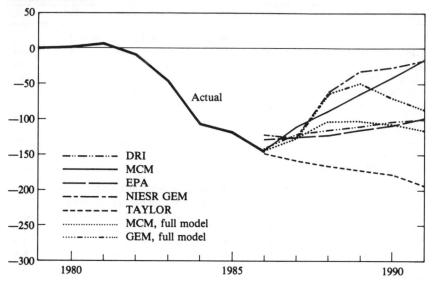

Figure V-2. *Scenario C: Real Net Exports of U.S. Goods and Services, Actual 1979–86 and Projected 1987–91*[a]

Billions of 1982 dollars

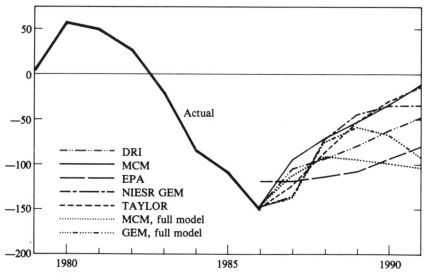

a. National income accounts basis.

Table V-3. *Scenario C: Total U.S. Merchandise Exports*
Percent deviation from scenario A

Model	1986	1987	1988	1989	1990	1991
			Volume			
DRI	0.0	1.8	3.4	5.6	8.2	10.6
EPA	0.0	3.0	5.7	8.1	10.9	13.8
MCM	0.0	3.5	5.1	7.9	10.2	12.6
NIESR GEM	0.0	1.5	2.3	3.4	4.1	4.6
OECD	n.a.	n.a.	n.a.	n.a.	n.a.	n.a.
TAYLOR[a]	0.0	0.9	1.9	3.0	4.1	5.3
MCM, full-model simulation	0.0	0.0	1.7	2.7	3.5	5.0
NIESR GEM, full-model simulation	0.0	0.6	2.4	5.5	9.5	12.8
			Price deflator			
DRI	0.0	0.0	0.3	0.8	1.5	2.2
EPA	0.0	−0.0	0.4	0.8	1.5	2.2
MCM	0.0	0.2	0.9	1.8	2.7	3.8
NIESR GEM	0.0	0.0	0.0	0.2	0.5	0.8
OECD	n.a.	n.a.	n.a.	n.a.	n.a.	n.a.
TAYLOR[a]	0.0	0.0	0.0	0.2	0.7	1.0
MCM, full-model simulation	0.0	0.0	0.3	0.7	1.1	1.6
NIESR GEM, full-model simulation	0.0	0.1	0.6	2.1	5.1	8.5

n.a. Not available.

a. TAYLOR model results are for goods and services rather than merchandise alone and are therefore not fully comparable with the results from the other models.

Table V-4. *Scenario C: Total U.S. Merchandise Imports*
Percent deviation from scenario A

Model	1986	1987	1988	1989	1990	1991
			Volume			
DRI	0.0	0.1	−0.3	−2.4	−5.2	−7.5
EPA	0.0	−0.1	−1.7	−4.8	−7.9	−10.5
MCM	0.0	−0.7	−4.0	−8.8	−13.4	−16.7
NIESR GEM	0.0	0.4	−0.5	−2.3	−5.7	−7.9
OECD	n.a.	n.a.	n.a.	n.a.	n.a.	n.a.
TAYLOR[a]	0.0	0.0	−1.3	−4.0	−7.0	−8.9
MCM, full-model simulation	0.0	0.0	−2.7	−5.2	−7.4	−8.1
NIESR GEM, full-model simulation	0.0	0.1	−0.1	3.7	8.7	12.9
			Price deflator			
DRI	0.0	−0.1	0.9	2.6	4.7	6.4
EPA	0.0	0.1	1.6	2.8	4.4	5.8
MCM	0.0	0.6	3.2	5.7	8.8	11.7
NIESR GEM	0.0	−0.1	0.5	1.1	2.0	2.6
OECD	n.a.	n.a.	n.a.	n.a.	n.a.	n.a.
TAYLOR[a]	0.0	−0.0	0.4	1.5	3.0	4.7
MCM, full-model simulation	0.0	0.0	1.0	3.1	5.4	7.7
NIESR GEM, full-model simulation	0.0	−0.1	0.9	2.6	5.7	8.6

n.a. Not available.
a. See note a to Annex table V-3.

Comparative Model Parameters

Model	Elasticity (long run)	Lag (years)[a] Mean	Maximum	Explanatory variable(s)
A. Income elasticity—nonoil imports				
DRI	1.2	0.3	1.0	Disaggregated domestic expenditure; output
EPA[b]	1.8	0.0	0.0	Real GNP
MCM	2.1	0.0	0.0	Real GNP
NIESR GEM	1.6	0.0	0.0	Total domestic expenditure
OECD	2.0	0.0	0.0	Disaggregated domestic expenditure; industrial production
TAYLOR[c]	2.5	0.2	*	Real GNP
B. Income elasticity—goods exports				
DRI	1.0	0.2	0.8	Industrial production for Canada, Japan, OECD Europe
EPA	1.2	0.0	0.0	Volume of world trade
MCM	2.1	0.0	0.0	Real GNP for the 4 countries in the model, weighted by shares in U.S. exports
NIESR GEM	1.0	0.0	0.0	Volume of world trade
OECD	1.0	0.0	0.0	Volume of world trade
TAYLOR[d]	1.3	0.8	*	Real GNP for 6 industrial countries
C. Price elasticity—nonoil imports				
DRI	1.1	0.6	1.25	Import deflator in national income accounts ÷ GNP deflator
EPA[b]	1.0	0.2	1.0	Import deflator in national income accounts ÷ inventory deflator
MCM	1.2	0.25	1.75	Import deflator in national income accounts ÷ GNP deflator
NIESR GEM	1.2	2.0	2.0	Index of foreign export prices for manufactures ÷ U.S. wholesale price index
OECD[e]	0.8	1.0	2.5	Unit value index for nonoil imports ÷ domestic expenditure deflator
TAYLOR[c]	0.7	0.2	*	Deflator for U.S. exports ÷ deflator for U.S. imports (national income accounts)
D. Price elasticity—goods exports				
DRI	0.72	0.7	2.0	Export deflator in national income accounts ÷ an index of prices for 15 industrial countries
EPA	0.79	0.25	2.0	Index of U.S. export prices ÷ an index of export prices for competitor countries
MCM	0.84	1.0	2.0	Export deflator in national income accounts ÷ an index of prices for 10 industrial countries and 8 developing countries
NIESR GEM	0.54	0.5	1.5	Unit value index for exports ÷ an index of competitors' prices
OECD	1.00	1.5	2.5	Unit value index for exports ÷ an index of competitors' prices
TAYLOR[d]	0.63	0.8	*	Deflator for U.S. exports ÷ deflator for U.S. imports (national income accounts)

Continued on next page

133

Section VI Table *(continued)*

Model	Elasticity (long run)	Lag (years)[a] Mean	Maximum	Explanatory variable(s)
E. Exchange rate elasticity—nonoil import price				
DRI	0.84	0.5	1.5	Weighted average for currencies of 15 industrial countries (Morgan Guaranty index)
EPA	0.50	0.0	0.0	Weighted average for currencies of 6 main competitor countries
MCM	0.91	0.25	1.75	Weighted average for currencies of 10 industrial countries and 8 developing countries (weights based on shares in U.S. imports)
NIESR GEM[f]	0.25	0.0	0.0	Weighted average for currencies of 11 competitor countries
OECD[g]	0.90	0.0	0.0	Weighted average for currencies of all countries
TAYLOR[c]	1.0	2.5	*	Weighted average for currencies of 6 industrial countries
F. Exchange rate elasticity—export price				
DRI	0.17	0.5	2.0	Weighted average for currencies of 15 industrial countries (Morgan Guaranty index)
EPA	0.20	0.0	0.0	Weighted average for currencies of 6 main competitor countries
MCM	0.23	0.0	0.75	Weighted average for currencies of 10 industrial countries and 8 developing countries (weights based on shares in U.S. imports)
NIESR GEM[h]	0.0	0.0	0.0	Weighted average for currencies of 11 competitor countries
OECD	0.6	0.5	1.0	Weighted average for currencies of all countries
TAYLOR[d]	0.0	0.0	0.0	Weighted average for currencies of 6 industrial countries

a. "*" denotes infinite lag; mean lag in this case is computed as $a/(1-a)$ where a is coefficient on lagged dependent variable. Mean lag for all the other models is computed as the amount of time in years it takes for half of the long-run effect to take place.

b. Includes oil prices.

c. Total imports of goods and services.

d. Total exports of goods and services.

e. Manufactured goods.

f. The 0.25 figure applies *only* if commodity prices stay fixed in dollars. Normally in GEM they will not, in which case the figure is about 0.55. See Simon Wren-Lewis, memorandum 5, "Workshop on the U.S. Current-Account Imbalance: Comparable Tables and Charts," Brookings Discussion Paper in International Economics 58, March 1987.

g. Manufactures and services; imposed coefficient.

h. If commodity prices change following a depreciation, as they normally would in GEM, the figure here should be about 0.25. The mean lag is probably near zero. See Simon Wren-Lewis, memorandum 5.

i. Average of elasticities for food, raw materials, energy, and manufactured goods, weighted by U.S. export shares.

Comparative Model Properties

THE FOLLOWING analysis outlines the comparative properties of the participating U.S. current-account models based on the results of the sensitivity analysis shocks presented in tables II-1 to II-6 and the parameters listed in the table in section VI. The analysis draws in part on memoranda prepared for the workshop by the participating modeling groups, and in part on the discussion that took place at the workshop.[1]

The table in section VI presents the income and price elasticities of merchandise export and nonoil import volumes, and the exchange rate elasticities of merchandise export and nonoil import prices, for each of the six participating models. The long-run elasticities (taking into account all lagged effects) are shown in the first column. The next two columns list the mean and maximum distributed lags on the elasticities (in years). The mean lag is defined as the number of years it takes to reach half of the full long-run impact. The last column identifies the explanatory variable in each model to which the elasticity estimate refers.

A *reduction of 1 percentage point in U.S. growth* results in a wide range of increases in the current account across the different models (table II-1). In all the models, U.S. income influences the current account through its effect on the volume of imports of goods and services. At one end of the spectrum, the TAYLOR model suggests that after five years (by 1991), the U.S. deficit would be reduced by 1.5 percent of GNP. At the other extreme, the NIESR GEM model shows an impact of less than 0.7 percent of GNP. The range of results obtained can be

---

1. The memoranda, which contain brief descriptions of the structures of each of the models, are available in "Workshop on the U.S. Current-Account Imbalance: Model Memoranda for DRI, EPA, NIESR (GEM), and TAYLOR," and "Workshop on the U.S. Current-Account Imbalance: Model Memoranda for Federal Reserve MCM, OECD, WHARTON," Brookings Discussion Papers in International Economics 59-A and 59-B, March 1987. A more complete description of the structure of the MCM's U.S. current-account sector is presented in chapter 2 of this book.

traced in part to differences in income elasticities of demand for nonoil imports (section VI table, panel A). The MCM and TAYLOR models, with relatively high income elasticities, also showed larger current-account effects than the other models. The NIESR GEM and DRI models were at the opposite end of the spectrum with relatively low income elasticities and small effects for a change in U.S. growth. The range of different income elasticities reflects to some degree differences in the income variables used in the equations—some models employ GNP and others use domestic expenditures. Although both the DRI and OECD models use disaggregated domestic expenditure variables, they yield income elasticities that differ widely (1.2 for the former and 2.0 for the latter). The DRI model includes trend terms in some of its import equations, which tend to reduce the income elasticities in those equations.

The variances in the sensitivity of the current account to U.S. growth across models also reflects differences in the treatment of services. Based on a comparison of the current-account and trade balance effects (in the top two panels of table II-1), the MCM shows a substantially greater sensitivity of net service receipts to the increase in U.S. growth than do the other models. The MCM is the only model in the group that specifies direct investment income payments explicitly as a function of growth (through its impact on profits). Unlike most of the other models, the MCM also takes into account feedbacks from increases in the current account to the stock of net foreign assets and income receipts on those assets. (The OECD model apparently does take into account feedbacks to asset stocks, and the DRI model does so indirectly by including a distributed lag on the current account in its factor income equations.)

An *increase of 1 percentage point in foreign growth* shows an even wider range of results (table II-2). The MCM again shows the largest impact: after five years, it is one and a half times the next highest estimate. Part of this difference can be attributed to the MCM's more complete modeling of the service account as described above—income receipts on U.S. direct investment abroad are particularly sensitive to GNP growth abroad. And the MCM's agricultural export prices are determined endogenously as a function of world income, among other factors, which contributes to the relatively greater expansion of the value of exports for that model. More fundamentally, the differences across models also reflect a wide range of estimates for the "income" elasticity of U.S. exports, as well as differences in the specification of income variables. The MCM's elasticity of 2.1 (for foreign GNP) is 60 percent greater than the next highest estimate (see panel B of section VI table). Most of the models have elasticities in the neighborhood of unity, but in most cases these unit elasticities are for the volume of world trade or foreign industrial production rather than foreign GNP. An effort was made to adjust for these specification differences in designing the simulation, by having world trade and foreign industrial production grow faster than foreign GNP. As shown in panel C of table II-2, differences in the growth of export volumes across models are somewhat less than the differences in income elasticities, but the differences in export volumes still account for much of the variance across models in the trade and current-account balance effects of the change in foreign growth.

The effects of a *2 percentage point decline in U.S. (and Eurodollar) interest rates* on the current account are shown in table II-3. The shift in interest rates was assumed not to affect any of the other "exogenous" determinants of the current account (namely, income, prices, or exchange rates) in this purely partial-equilibrium exercise, with two exceptions as noted below. Dollar interest rates influence the current account directly through portfolio income payments and receipts, since most U.S. portfolio claims on foreigners, as well as liabilities to foreigners, are denominated in dollars. The DRI, EPA, MCM, and OECD models all specify investment or factor income receipts and payments separately as functions of interest rates. These models show effects in a range of 0.22 to 0.37 percent of GNP after five years. The varying effects reflect differences in estimated parameters rather than differences in baseline asset stocks, since only one model (the MCM) includes asset stocks explicitly in the determination of investment income flows. Nevertheless, the generally positive effects of the decline in interest rates are consistent with the substantial and growing net foreign liability position of the United States in dollar-denominated portfolio assets in the baseline period.

The TAYLOR model, which does not include interest rates in its determination of aggregate imports and exports of goods and services, is one of the exceptions referred to above, in that interest rates influence other determinants of net exports. This model's current-account sector includes equations relating exchange rates to interest rates, and the simulation was run with exchange rates treated endogenously. The small increase in the current account reported for the TAYLOR model reflects a depreciation of the dollar that resulted from lower U.S. interest rates. The EPA model also reported a simulation in which exchange rates were treated endogenously; the effect on the current account was substantially greater than with the exchange rate held exogenous. The difference between the two results reported by the EPA shows a substantially greater sensitivity to the induced impact on the exchange rate than was the case for the TAYLOR model. This result is consistent with the differences observed in the responses of those two models to the exogenous exchange rate shocks (discussed below). The NIESR GEM model, which does not include the U.S. service account, reported no effect for the interest rate shock.

Table II-4 shows the effects of a *1 percentage point reduction in U.S. inflation*. Lower U.S. inflation improves the current account in real terms by reducing the price of exports relative to foreign prices and by raising the relative price of imports. This stimulus to the volume of net exports is partly offset in nominal terms by the reduction of export prices. In some cases the decline in U.S. prices also has a significant negative impact on import prices. The models show fairly broad agreement that the level of export prices will be reduced by something like 4 to 5 percent after five years as a result of the decline in U.S. inflation. This finding suggests that changes in domestic prices are passed through fairly completely to export prices. There are sharp differences about the implications for import prices, however. In the NIESR GEM model, U.S. domestic prices have a predominant direct influence on import prices. In the DRI and OECD models, there is a small but noticeable direct impact, and in the EPA, MCM, and TAYLOR models, there is no discernible effect. (Most of the models do allow for a transitory indirect effect, as noted below in the discussion of the exchange rate shock.)

All the models show significant reductions in import volume and significant increases in export volume in response to lower U.S. inflation. Most of the models have price elasticities in the neighborhood of unity, with import and export elasticities summing to between 1.7 and 2.0 in all cases but one. The TAYLOR model has price elasticities that sum to 1.3, and compared with most of the other models, it shows a noticeably smaller impact of U.S. inflation on trade volumes and the current account.

Table II-5 shows the impact of a *20 percent depreciation of the dollar against all other currencies*. The simulation was run under the hypothetical assumption, known to be false in some cases, that all other determinants of the current account (for example, incomes, domestic prices, and interest rates) would not be affected by the exchange rate change. In the models, a depreciation tends to raise import prices and to a lesser extent export prices, reduce import volumes, and stimulate export volumes. The net impact on the current account after five years ranges from a low of 0.3 percent of GNP for the TAYLOR model, to a high of 2.7 percent of GNP for the MCM model. The TAYLOR model estimate is at the low end because it has a combination of relatively low import and export price elasticities (hence a low increase in real net exports) and no increase in export prices in response to the depreciation. The MCM is at the high end of the spectrum, in part because its price elasticities, particularly for imports, are higher than the price elasticities in most of the other models. (The import price elasticity is especially relevant because the scale of imports is substantially greater than that of exports in the baseline.) The NIESR GEM model also has a relatively high price elasticity for imports, but it has the lowest elasticity for exports and it excludes services. The DRI, MCM, and OECD results all suggest that the depreciation affected the service account significantly (compare panels A and B). The EPA model's current-account impact is depressed relative to the others inasmuch as the denominator in its relative export price term (foreign export prices) was treated endogenously. This meant that the depreciation affected the relative price of exports (hence export volume and value) relatively less than in other models. Reasons for the relatively low current-account and trade balance effects registered by the OECD model are not immediately apparent, although its import price elasticity is at the low end of the range.

As shown in table II-5, panel F, all but one of the models indicates that a 20 percent depreciation eventually will be largely but not fully passed through into higher import prices. (Full pass-through would imply a 25 percent rise in prices, whereas most of the models fall in a range of 19–22 percent.) In most cases some lag is involved, suggesting that competition with U.S. producers significantly affects import prices (and foreign profit margins) at least temporarily. Unlike the other models, the OECD model shows immediate and full pass-through, while the NIESR GEM model shows a much smaller impact than the others. In the latter case, import prices are determined largely by U.S. domestic prices and are influenced to a much lesser extent by foreign prices and exchange rates. Most of the models also agree that a depreciation would have a moderate, positive effect on export prices, although the NIESR GEM and TAYLOR models show no impact.

In all the models, when the *dollar depreciates against just the yen and the EMS currencies* (table II-6), the effects are noticeably smaller than for an across-the-board depreciation.

Workshop Participants and Observers

with their affiliations at the time of the workshop

Tam Bayoumi *Stanford University*
Richard Berner *Salomon Brothers*
Barry P. Bosworth *Brookings Institution*
James M. Boughton *International Monetary Fund*
Ralph C. Bryant *Brookings Institution*
Nigel Gault *Data Resources Incorporated*
John Green *Wharton Econometrics Forecasting Associates*
Richard Haas *International Monetary Fund*
William L. Helkie *Federal Reserve Board*
John F. Helliwell *University of British Columbia*
Dale W. Henderson *Georgetown University*
Gerald Holtham *Brookings Institution*
Peter Hooper *Federal Reserve Board*
Howard J. Howe *Wharton Econometrics Forecasting Associates*
Peter Isard *International Monetary Fund*
Paul R. Krugman *Massachusetts Institute of Technology*
Robert Z. Lawrence *Brookings Institution*
Catherine L. Mann *Federal Reserve Board*
Stephen Marris *Institute for International Economics*
Paul Masson *International Monetary Fund*
Brian Mulaney *Morgan Stanley*
Pete Richardson *Organization for Economic Cooperation and Development*
Robert Solomon *Brookings Institution*
Steven A. Symansky *World Bank*
Ralph Tryon *Federal Reserve Board*
Simon Wren-Lewis *National Institute of Economic and Social Research, London*

Naohiro Yashiro *Economic Research Institute, Japanese Economic Planning Agency*

Paul Armington *World Bank*

Jason Benderly *Goldman Sachs and Company*

C. Fred Bergsten *Institute for International Economics*

Matthew Canzoneri *Georgetown University*

Gerard Caprio *Morgan Guaranty Trust*

Donald Curtis *U.S. Treasury Department*

William Dewald *U.S. Department of State*

Stephen Dunaway *International Monetary Fund*

Robert Eckley *Brookings Institution Visiting Fellow*

Craig Elwell *Congressional Research Service*

Carol Evans *Brookings Institution*

Geza Feketekuty *Office of the U.S. Special Trade Representative*

Harvey Galper *Brookings Institution*

Morris Goldstein *International Monetary Fund*

Jane Haltmaier *Federal Reserve Board*

Andrea Hodson *Brookings Institution*

Gregory Hoelscher *Chase Manhattan Bank*

Gary Hufbauer *Georgetown University*

Greg Hume *Brookings Institution*

Shafiqul Islam *Institute for International Economics*

John Jelacic *U.S. Department of Commerce*

Giles Keating *Credit Suisse First Boston*

Barbara Koremenos *Brookings Institution*

Malcolm D. Knight *International Monetary Fund*

Flemming Larsen *International Monetary Fund*

Michael Leahy *Federal Reserve Board*

William Lee *Federal Reserve Board*

Frank Levy *Brookings Institution Guest Scholar*

Edward F. McKelvey *Goldman Sachs and Company*

Jaime Marquez *Federal Reserve Board*

Ellen Meade *Federal Reserve Board*

Kathryn Morisse *Federal Reserve Board*
David Morrison *Goldman Sachs International Corporation*
Ellen Nedde *Brookings Institution*
Robert Nicholson *U.S. Department of Commerce*
Gus O'Donnell *British Embassy*
James Reitzes *Federal Reserve Bank of New York*
Walter S. Salant *Brookings Institution*
Lois Stekler *Federal Reserve Board*
Stephen Thurman *Congressional Budget Office*
David Walters *Office of the U.S. Special Trade Representative*
Takashi Watanabe *Brookings Institution Guest Scholar*
Paul Wonnacott *University of Maryland*

Index

Agricultural exports, 24, 30
Asset stocks, 29, 43–44

Bacchetta, Philippe, 88n
Baldwin, Richard E., 53, 64n, 97
Bryant, Ralph C., 3n, 49
Budget balance changes, 45
Budget deficit reduction, 76, 77, 80

Capacity utilization, 23, 25
Combined-model projection, 65–67, 69
Conditional projections, 65–67, 69–71
Constant price balance, 65–67
Current account: agricultural exports, 24,
    30; exchange rate effects, 46, 95–97;
    external investment position, 12,
    14–15; fiscal shock simulations, 46–51,
    109–15; foreign fiscal expansion ef-
    fects, 46–49, 127–32; growth and, 35,
    37, 40–42, 44; historical performance,
    12, 14–17; multicountry model simula-
    tions, 46–51; nonagricultural exports,
    38–39, 42; nonoil imports, 38, 42; oil
    imports, 24, 30; price change factors,
    37–39, 42; U.S. fiscal contraction
    effects, 46–51, 121–26. See also Invest-
    ment income; Merchandise trade
    balance; Trade balance
Current-account model (chap. 2), 17–18,
    20; balances and asset stocks treat-
    ment, 29; investment income, 27, 29,
    35; predictive performance, 30, 35;
    services, 27, 29, 35; trade prices, 24–
    25, 27, 30; trade volumes, 20–21,
    23–24, 30
Current-price balance, 65–67, 69

Data Resources Inc. (DRI) model, 3,
    61–62. See also Multicountry models
Debt-GNP ratio, 90–94
Debt servicing, 69, 73, 87
Demand growth, 40–41, 58, 61, 71, 72,
    78–80
Direct investment income, 14–15, 27, 35,
    44
Domestic demand. See Demand growth

Edison, Hali J., 20n, 87n
Exchange rate: current account and, 46,
    95–97; deficit and, 11–12, 58, 62–64,
    70–71; fiscal shocks and, 46, 48, 49;
    indexes, 51–52, 89, 96; interest rates
    and, 89–91, 94, 97–98; international
    cooperation and, 75, 77, 78–79; predic-
    tion inadequacy, 62; price competi-
    tiveness and, 51–52; prices and, 11–12,
    15, 23–25, 27, 37–38; projections and,
    65–66; recession risk and, 73; service
    accounts and, 15
Exchange rate sustainability, 82–83;
    calculation of, 90–94; conceptual
    approaches, 84–86; current-account
    balance and, 95–97; debt financing fac-
    tors, 86–87; 1986–87 experience, 87–89
External investment position, 12, 14–15

Federal Reserve Board Multicountry
    Model (MCM), 3, 18, 46–49, 61, 87.
    See also Multicountry models
Feedbacks, 4, 29
Feldstein, Martin, 88n
Fiscal policy, 11, 45, 48–50, 77–80
Fiscal shock simulations, 5, 46–51,
    109–15

145